"Since all Scripture is breathed out by God, I find it helpful to restate a verse about God as if God Himself is speaking about Himself. Vic Black has taken this concept to a new and deeper level in his treatment of entire Psalms as if God Himself is speaking. This book will encourage anyone who wants to develop a more personal relationship with God."

JERRY BRIDGES
Bestselling author

"Follow Vic Black into the Psalms as he fleshes out an exercise to slow you down. Ponder a psalm with fresh eyes; engage a sanctified imagination and an upturned ear—listening for God's voice, listening for how Jesus might personalize the Psalms to you."

JEAN FLEMING
Author of *Pursue the Intentional Life*

"Vic Black has been a friend and a mentor in prayer for me for many years. He is a man who lives what he teaches. The concept of Psalms in the first person is one that will accelerate every person's prayer life and their engagement with the Lord Jesus. Grab a copy—it will put a fresh wind in your prayer life."

DOUG NUENKE
President of The Navigators

"Every now and then you meet someone who you sense really knows Jesus—who doesn't just know *about* Jesus but has really experienced Him intimately. Vic Black is one of those people. As he walks us through the Psalms, I sense being in the presence of the Lord. Join Vic as you walk closely together in God's presence!"

LAUREN LIBBY
International president/CEO of TWR International (Trans World Radio)

"God spoke His Word; God speaks through His Word. Yet in a very loud world, it can be hard to hear His voice. Vic Black wants to change that. Here he offers a fresh new method of engaging with God through the Scriptures. Join Vic on a very special journey into a variety of psalms— reading each one, waiting upon the Lord, listening for His voice, expecting to hear from Him. Enjoy the Lord and His Word and go ever deeper with the God who still speaks."

DEAN RIDINGS
Author of *The Pray! Prayer Journal*

"Through personalizing the Psalms, Vic lays out a path to engage God that breathes new understanding into the Word of God being living and active. The Scriptures were written to encourage us so that we have hope (Romans 15:4), and this book makes that encouragement and hope accessible. Vic offers us a means of regaining a sense of wonder as we hear the Father speak into our lives and circumstances. Whether you struggle with the feeling that God is distant and only tolerates you or you delight in an increasing hunger for Him, this book will shake your foundations."

THE RT. REV. KEN ROSS
Missionary Bishop with the Anglican Church of Rwanda

"Prayer starts not when we speak to God but when God speaks to us. Prayer is His initiative. When we respond, we join a conversation that is eternal. Dietrich Bonhoeffer wrote, 'The richness of the Word of God ought to determine our prayer, not the poverty of our heart.' Vic Black has harnessed the power of these ideas in *Speak, Lord*. Placing selected psalms in first person and teaching us to do the same, this book is a sharpened tool for personal devotions, small-group prayer, and leadership training."

CHIP JACKSON
Teaching pastor at Fellowship Bible Church in northwest Arkansas

"The most authentic words ever written are those that originate from God. Vic had been praying for new insights in Psalm 23 when the thought was given him to see this psalm as though it were written in first person . . . as though God Himself were speaking these words to him. The question may arise: 'How can I trust that these thoughts came from God to Vic?' Several of us who know Vic have testified that he is trustworthy. Vic's life is evidence of his deep relationship with God. You can trust what Vic has written. He is passing on to us what God gave him. As the psalms have come alive for Vic, they can come alive for you. I highly endorse this book."

LEE BRASE
Founder of The Navigators Prayer Ministry and author of *Praying from God's Heart* and *Approaching God*.

"I have always started my daily devotions reading a psalm. But Vic Black has stirred me to a deeper experience with the Psalms. This book is not a theology but a practicum on how to worship with the worship book of all time, the Psalms. He shows us how and leads us in doing it, not just thinking about it. This is powerful and life changing."

JERRY WHITE, PhD
Major General, USAF, retired; The Navigators International President Emeritus; and coauthor of *To Be a Friend* and *Honesty, Morality, and Conscience*

Speak, Lord

Speak, Lord

Hearing Psalms in the First Person

Vic Black

A NavPress resource published in alliance
with Tyndale House Publishers, Inc.

NAVPRESS⬤®

NavPress is the publishing ministry of The Navigators, an international Christian organization and leader in personal spiritual development. NavPress is committed to helping people grow spiritually and enjoy lives of meaning and hope through personal and group resources that are biblically rooted, culturally relevant, and highly practical.

For more information, visit www.NavPress.com.

Speak, Lord: Hearing Psalms in the First Person

Copyright © 2015 by Victor Black. All rights reserved.

A NavPress resource published in alliance with Tyndale House Publishers, Inc.

NAVPRESS and the NAVPRESS logo are registered trademarks of NavPress, The Navigators, Colorado Springs, CO. TYNDALE is a registered trademark of Tyndale House Publishers, Inc. Absence of ® in connection with marks of NavPress or other parties does not indicate an absence of registration of those marks.

Cover design by Mark Anthony Lane II.
Cover photograph copyright © Luke Gram/Stocksy.com. All rights reserved.

The Word Hand illustration copyright © 1964 The Navigators. Used by permission of The Navigators. All rights reserved.

Some of the anecdotal illustrations in this book are true to life and are included with the permission of the persons involved. All other illustrations are composites of real situations, and any resemblance to people living or dead is coincidental.

Cataloging-in-Publication Data is available.

ISBN 978-1-63146-370-9

Printed in the United States of America

21	20	19	18	17	16	15
7	6	5	4	3	2	1

To my dear wife, Lindy, who exemplifies a life of probing curiosity in the Scriptures and intimacy with the Lord. Your heart for God has always been a challenge for me to emulate. Keep setting the bar high, Sweetheart. I'll try to keep up.

Contents

Foreword

EVERYONE PRAYS—KIND OF. It is our most human action. At the deep center of our lives, we are connected somehow or other to God. That deep center often gets buried under everyday debris of routine and distraction and chatter, while we shuffle about, out of touch and unaware of our true selves. Then a sudden jolt opens a crevasse, exposing for a moment our bedrock self: spontaneously we pray. We pray because it is our most human response. We are made by and for the voice of God—listening to and answering that voice is our most characteristic act. We are most ourselves when we pray.

The jolt comes variously—a stab of pain, a rush of beauty, an encore of joy; we exclaim, "God!" The cry can be complaint or curse or praise; no matter, it is prayer. When that deep, deep center of our lives is exposed—our core humanity, which biblical writers so vigorously designate as "heart"—we unthinkingly revert to our first language: we pray.

The Psalms are the prayerbook of the Bible. When people ask their fellow Christian, "Teach me to pray," the traditional response has been to introduce them to the Psalms. Jesus prayed the Psalms; how can we improve on Jesus? Vic Black, who heads up the prayer ministry of The Navigators, in that capacity, has been praying the Psalms for much of his life. But at one point he ventured out in a fresh way, by praying the Psalms in the first person. He got his start in Psalm 23, one of the most familiar of the Psalms. We are used to reading "The Lord is my shepherd . . ." Vic Black personalizes it into the first person: "I, the LORD—I am your Shepherd. You have no need of anything because I am all you need . . ."

Vic Black's counsel to pray the Psalms in the first person, listening to God address us in the first person has its precedence early in the biblical story in Moses. God became present to Moses as he was tending his flock in the Midian wilderness. A burning bush that didn't burn up caught Moses' attention; he approached the bush to see what was going on. God spoke Moses' name from the flames of the bush: "Moses, Moses." Conversation between God and Moses developed. God announced his intention to deliver his people from Egyptian slavery and told Moses that he wanted him to lead them out to "a good and broad land." Moses was reluctant but after a lengthy back-and-forth exchange agreed. He received his instructions, and the action was launched (Exodus 3–4).

Then Moses asked God to identify Himself: "When my people ask me Your name, what shall I tell them? There are a lot of gods out there—what is *Your* name?"

God said to Moses, "I AM THAT I AM. Tell them, 'I AM has sent me to you.' . . . That is My name forever" (Exodus 3:13-15, author's paraphrase).

I AM THAT I AM—God's name for Himself—tells Moses that God is alive, present to him, and ready to enact salvation. This God-revealed name—and the understandings that developed as it was used in prayer and obedience by the Hebrew people—marks the deconstruction of every kind and sort of impersonal, magical, manipulative, abstract, coercive way of understanding God. Listening to and answering I AM THAT I AM placed the Hebrew people as participating witnesses in the grand historical drama of salvation that challenges and brings about the eventual dissolution of every counter way of life, the world principalities and powers against which Paul would later issue a call to arms (Ephesians 6:10-20), "all the kingdoms of the world and their splendor" that Jesus refused to bargain for with the devil (Matt. 4:8-10, NIV). Worshiping I AM THAT I AM developed into a way of life in Israel in which love defined relationship—all of them, no exceptions: God, neighbor, stranger, enemy, family. Serving and obeying I AM THAT I AM became an exploration in all the dimensions of freedom: freedom from sin and oppression and damnation.

I AM THAT I AM—this verb-dominated, relational, emphatic sentence by which God willed to be understood—was shortened to a verbal noun of four letters, YHWH, probably pronounced Yahweh (and usually translated LORD in English). It became the primary term among the Hebrews for address and reference to the self-revealing God of Israel, used 6,700 times in the Old Testament as compared to the 2,500 occurrences of the generic Semitic term for divinity, Elohim (translated into English simply as "God").

The name spoken from the burning bush marked the definitive revelation of God as present to us and personal with us—God here among us, a living God in relation with us. No more gods of sticks and stones. No more gods to be appeased or bribed or courted. No more gods decked out in abstractions for philosophical speculation. No more gods cast as major players in cosmic war and sex myth dramas.

A millennium plus a couple of centuries later, Jesus continued and then completed the event at the bush; He took these very words, these I AM words on His lips, and fleshed them out in salvation meetings and salvation conversations with lost and dying, confused and bedeviled, sick and guilty slaves of sin, and led them into a new life. Famously, the seven Jesus I AM self-identifications in John's Gospel (bread of life—6:35; light of the world—8:12; gate for the sheep—10:7; good shepherd—10:11; the resurrection and the life—11:25; the way the truth and the life—14:6; the vine—15:1) place God's personal, first-person voice into our lives.

I find it energizing to place myself alongside Moses at the burning bush and alongside Jesus in Galilee and Jerusalem as I listen to God speaking to me in the first person from the Psalms.

Eugene H. Peterson
Translator of *The Message*
Professor Emeritus of Spiritual Theology, Regent College, BC

Introduction

I speak to thirsty hearts whose longings have been wakened by the touch of God within them, and such as they need no reasoned proof. Their restless hearts furnish all the proof they need. ... I am addressing the thirsting souls who are determined to follow God. ... The urge of God within them will assure their continuing pursuit.

A. W. TOZER, *The Pursuit of God*

WHY DO YOU READ THE PSALMS? Do you expect to hear God speak? Are you listening?

I once met a young businessman who had not been raised in a family that valued the Bible or Christianity—his dad was an atheist, and his mom was a non-practicing Jew. But one day his workplace mentor suggested, "You should read the Bible. Everyone needs to read the Bible sometime." So he went to Costco and bought his first Bible—and read half of it! *If this stuff is reliable and believable,* he thought, *I'm going to have to make some adjustments.* He did sufficient research to satisfy himself that the Bible was in fact reliable and believable. And he believed!

"What's your Bible reading like today?" I asked him.

"I don't read the Bible," he replied, then paused. "I listen to it." When he engages with the words on the pages of Scripture, he is listening, expecting to hear from God.

Listening to God is at the heart of this book. In the Psalms, God captures the essence of the complex human experience, the extensive drama of mankind—from the depths of despair and frustration to the heights of elation. Most of us find comfort and courage from the psalmists' intimate engagement with the Only True Living God, but I have found that the more I read the Psalms, the more I am drawn into the heart of God with a childlike declaration: "I want some of that!" I want to taste the relationship I see demonstrated between David and his God. I want to soar to the heights. I want to find God in the depths.

Through my years of probing the Psalms, God has been incredibly generous, fulfilling my desire for more of Him. And He extends the same invitation to you. Are you hungry for more of God? Does your heart cry for a deeper, richer taste of Him from the Psalms? I am convinced He is ready to satisfy.

I cannot take credit for the probing question at the heart of this book: "What would it sound like if God spoke this particular psalm to me in the first person?" I'm not sure I ever would have come up with such a wonder-filled inquiry on my own. All credit goes to the God who invades our standard, sometimes mundane attempts to know Him, initiating relationship with us. This book is the exposed heart of a God-seeker sharing his vulnerable engagement with his Friend, his Comforter, his Savior, his Mighty Warrior, his Good Shepherd.

My Journey into the Psalms

It was October. We were in the beautiful Adirondack Mountains of New York, where I had been invited to facilitate a prayer retreat for college students. The setting was serene: a big cabin tucked next to a crystal lake, surrounded by trees alive with brilliant colors.

As our retreat group began to focus on God through worship, Scripture, our own prayers, and silence, He led us to the Shepherd/sheep relationship we share with Him. John 10 and Psalm 23 were key passages that we explored slowly and deeply in prayer. Someone pointed out the emphasis on God in Psalm 23: "*He* is my shepherd, *He* makes me lie down, *He* leads me, *He* restores me, *He* guides me, *He* is with me, *His* rod and staff comfort me, *He* prepares a table, *He* anoints my head." We were all stunned by this clarification and powerful emphasis on the Shepherd. God was pulling back the curtain to show us a glimpse of His heart, letting us know loud and clear that our lives and well-being are completely tied up in Him.

God made it clear in John 10:3-5 that His sheep (that's us) hear His voice and follow Him: "The sheep hear his voice, and he calls his own sheep by name. . . . The sheep follow him because they know his voice. . . . They do not know the voice of strangers." As I soaked in John 10, I concluded that perhaps our Shepherd wanted to speak to each of us, and I suggested we all spend some time alone with Him. I soon found my own rock by the lake and settled in to listen to the Shepherd of my soul (1 Peter 2:25).

I am by nature a very optimistic person, but as I gathered my Bible and journal beside the lake in the Adirondacks, I had a slightly pessimistic thought: *I'm probably not going to get anything new out of Psalm 23.* After all, I had spent extensive time exploring the Shepherd Psalm through the years. But in the next few moments, as I stilled my heart and mind before God, something changed. It was as though the Lord, the Shepherd Himself, showed up.

I could sense Him standing there, looking over my shoulder

with a slight smile on His face. "So you don't think you're going to get anything new out of Psalm 23, huh?" He asked. I felt a little embarrassed. Then the most amazing thing happened. The Lord began to speak Psalm 23 to me in the first person. The Shepherd, Jesus, was speaking of Himself! I was writing as fast as I could, attempting to capture all He was saying. I can honestly say I was not thinking and processing Psalm 23 on my own. I was simply writing what the Shepherd said. His words flowed like cool water and tasted like the sweetest honey:

PSALM 23 IN THE FIRST PERSON

I, the LORD*—I am your Shepherd. You have no need of anything because I am all you need. I will lead you to green pastures and cause you to lie down. I will lead you to quiet waters, to waters of rest, and cause you to drink your fill. I am very serious about your rest and restoration. I will even restore your soul. I will guide you, not push you, down the particular path of righteousness, for the sake of My name. You will know this is the right path because you will see My tracks, My footprints of righteousness and holiness right in front of you. When I say so, together we will leave this quiet and restful place and go to other places that are not so restful. Some of these places may be scary. Some will be places of deep darkness and even death. But don't be afraid; I'm with you. My footprints are still right in front of you. My rod and My staff will touch you during those dark and scary times to keep you on the path and to reassure you of My presence. I may even prepare a table before you right in front of your enemies. But remember, I'm right there, too! I will anoint your head with My oil. It's My oil of authority and recognition as well as My oil of healing for your wounds. Your cup will run over with Me, with My very presence! You will become more and more convinced that My goodness and My lovingkindness will aggressively pursue you for your entire lifetime. You will also become more and more* *convinced that you will live comfortably in My house for all the length of your days—not only on this earth, but in eternity! I love you. You are that little lamb on My shoulders.*

I was stunned. Had God really spoken this to me? Had He invaded my quiet spot in the Adirondacks to introduce a beautiful new method of engaging with Him in the Psalms?

The Process

Right away I started a special journal dedicated to experiencing psalms in the first person with the Lord. As I began to experiment receiving other psalms in this fashion, several principles soon fell into place.

Listening

Receiving psalms in the first person is much more a listening exercise than a writing exercise. In most cases, I don't write anything for a while. But there are other times when I start writing right away. There certainly is no exact formula to follow, and there are no grades given here. Enjoying the relationship is more important than doing something right or wrong. Learn to rest and relax in the presence of God, engaging your heart with His heart, receiving from Him words of love, affirmation, strength, and identity. So please, if you do anything in learning this process, enjoy the Lord. And believe that you are being enjoyed by Him.

All you currently know to be true about God supports your experience of listening to Him speak the psalm to you personally. Remember, we are not rewriting Scripture. There is only one infallible Word of God. This exercise of personalizing psalms is intended to open our hearts to hear His voice from Scripture. As you listen to the Lord, I encourage you to examine what you believe you are hearing against Scripture and in the context of a trusted community of friends. What you think you are hearing from the Psalms should line up with the strong truth of Scripture.

As you enter this meditative exercise, I would suggest praying something like, "Lord, I don't want to put words in Your mouth. I don't want my imagination to run away with me either. But I do want to engage my imagination, as well as my heart, my soul, my mind, and all of my faculties. What I want more than anything is to truly hear Your voice. Would You give me ears to hear? Would You block out all distractions?"

Studying

If possible, I would encourage you to have several Bible translations available and open. One reason for this is that wonderful and extensive work has gone into each translation to expand the original meaning of every verse. Observe the footnotes, definitions, and cross references that further unlock the meaning of the passage. In verse 3 of Psalm 23, my New American Standard Bible gives a footnote for the phrase "paths of righteousness." For the word *path*, the footnote is, "Literally, 'track.'" This word really piqued my curiosity.

A path through the woods is normally created from many people traveling the same trail. When the path is first being established, the trail may be faint, hard to discern and follow. But as more and more people travel the path, adding their footprints— their "tracks"—to the trail, the path becomes clearer and more distinct. The grass and other foliage have difficulty growing due to the foot traffic. When I thought about this in the context of Psalm 23, I considered who had left these "tracks," these footprints of righteousness. It had to be the Holy One, the Shepherd Himself. Hence, I rendered this phrase, "You will know this is the right path because you will see My tracks, My footprints of righteousness and holiness right in front of you." So even through the footnotes of our Bibles, God extends Himself to us for deeper relationship.

Often when I ask the question, "Lord, what would it sound like if You spoke this psalm to me personally?" God begins to bring other Scripture into focus, adding color and dimension to the psalm I'm examining. Certain phrases from Scripture begin to come to life: "Let the word of Christ richly dwell within you" (Colossians 3:16); "If you abide in Me, and My words abide in you" (John 15:7); "For the word of God is living and active" (Hebrews 4:12). The Holy Spirit weaves Scripture tucked away in your heart to reveal deeper meaning in the psalm you are currently living in. So if you hope for this to be more than a literary exercise, it's essential that you live a life saturated with God's Word. God will pull phrases and verses from your heart to enhance the psalm you are working on.

Waiting

There is freedom and peace in waiting, listening, and soaking in a psalm. Allow God to speak. Trust Him. Give yourself permission to listen and not put words in God's mouth. He doesn't need our help to speak. If God moved men by the power of the Holy Spirit, causing them to write what He wanted them to write (2 Peter 1:21), then He certainly can speak to us creatively from the Psalms. Since one of His preferred names is the Word (John 1:1), I would expect Him to present Himself as the God who continues to speak to His people, drawing us into increasing conversation and intimacy.

Picture the Lord with you in the context of your time alone with Him as you ask this question. Wait for His answer. You may be in a coffee shop. Can you envision Him sitting next to you as you read? You may be walking in the woods. Can you sense Him walking with you, joining your thoughts as you reflect on a psalm? You may be in a foxhole or some other stressful and potentially dangerous environment. Experience the Lord right there with you, speaking words of comfort, protection, and perspective. In any and every case, listen to Him. The truth is, He really is with you all the time! He makes this promise to you over and over in Scripture: "Never will I leave you; never will I forsake you" (Hebrews 13:5, NIV; see also Deuteronomy 31:6); "Surely I am with you always [literally "all the days"], to the very end of the age" (Matthew 28:20, NIV). Nothing can snatch you out of God's hand (John 10:27-30). Nothing—absolutely nothing—can separate you from God's love (Romans 8:38, 39).

I would encourage you to live in one psalm for a period of time. The objective is not speed. I would not encourage you to try to do one psalm a day. Take a slower approach and stay in a psalm for a week or two. The Psalms flowed out of David's life (as well as the lives of Moses, Asaph, Solomon, and the sons of Korah). As you seek to let the Psalms to flow out of your Bible and into your life, you may spend hours or even days reflecting, meditating, soaking, and marinating in a favorite psalm. Let the psalm live. Let it breathe. Let it live in you. Let God speak. Then write your impressions.

Here are some thoughts to keep in mind as you experiment with receiving psalms in the first person:

» Relax. Enjoy the experience. This is much more a heart exercise than a head exercise. View your practice as fun and relational time with God.

» Your question is simply, "Lord, what would it sound like if You spoke this psalm to me personally?" You may be more comfortable with the question, "Lord, what *might* it sound like if You spoke this psalm to me personally?" *Might* may help you not think in terms of a right and wrong way of doing it. Remember, what you "think" you are hearing from the Psalms should line up with His Word.

» Read meditatively in several translations. Allow the footnotes and cross references to add color and meaning to the psalm.

» Soak in one psalm. Allow fresh, new phrases to form in your heart and mind. Allow your sanctified imagination to soar and expand the psalm.

» Work on one complete thought at a time. Don't force it.

» Allow God to take your pen and add His personalized phrases. Listen to the Lord speak these thoughts to your heart.

» Compare what you have heard to what you know of God from Scripture. Discuss your psalm in the first person with your friends. Once you have finished the psalm, read it over and over. Hear it and receive it as the Lord's blessing to you.

The Process in Action

To illustrate some of the ways God works in this process, I want to give two examples of psalms in the first person from my journal. Psalm 24 has grown to be quite special to me because God took me way outside the box and entered dramatically into my real-life circumstances. Psalm 18 expresses God's passionate heart of protection for His kids when they cry out for help. May these two psalms help to provide a foundation as you further explore this book.

Let God Take the Pen

Occasionally, as I'm listening to the Lord and writing, God seems to take my pen and add a few lines outside my box, invading my psalm exercise to add color, truth, and deeper relational experience.

As I meditated on some of the phrases in Psalm 24, questions for clarification and deeper probing began to enter my thoughts. Verse 7: "Lift up your heads, O you gates, and be lifted up, O ancient doors, that the King of glory may come in!" Where has He been? Why is the King of glory outside the gates, returning to the protective environments of the city walls? Perhaps the answer is in verse 8: "The LORD strong and mighty, the LORD mighty in battle." He's been out fighting a recent battle!

Meditating further on this spectacle of the King of glory returning from His latest battle, my sanctified imagination began to paint a picture. I could see Jesus riding a great white horse at the front of a celebratory parade. His mighty warriors followed close behind, rejoicing with those inside the gate over their victory. I saw myself eagerly watching at the edge of the street as the King and His fighting force triumphantly rode back into the city. Confetti was flying! Horns were blaring! Everyone was shouting and rejoicing because our King had won a new battle. I craned my neck to get a better view as the King approached.

When the King was right in front of me, He stopped. He pulled up His royal steed and looked right at me. It was as though the entire parade and celebration faded into the background because the King was focusing on me. He leaned down from His stamping stallion and spoke to me quietly, so no one else could hear.

"It was your battle," He said.

"M-m-my battle?" I stammered. "I didn't know I had a battle."

He replied with a smile, "I know. The enemy had set an ambush for you. They may have finally defeated you with their strategy this time. But I destroyed their snare. You're safe now. Enjoy the celebration."

I was stunned. Could it be that I have battles I know nothing about? Certainly I am very aware of those battles I'm in the midst of, fighting furiously against the enemy, fully clothed in the armor of God. But could there be battles, ambushes, strategies set for me that God goes before me to demolish and dismantle? I was safe inside the city walls, and the King of glory was outside fighting my battle for me. I was humbled, but I was very glad.

PSALM 24 IN THE FIRST PERSON

Look around you. Do you see the earth and everything in the earth? It's all Mine. Everyone who lives here, they're Mine too. I founded the earth. I built it. I established the land and the waters. Who in the world can come up My holy mountain? Who would dare ascend My holy hill? Who could possibly stand in My holy place? I'll tell you who. The one whose hands are not defiled. The one whose heart is open and examined by Me. The one who has Me high and lifted up, and nothing else and no one else shares that place with Me. The one who does not manipulate others to get their own way. The one who responds with humility and sorrow when I bring conviction for their sin. This kind of person will receive a blessing from Me. I will lock eyes with them and smile full in their face. They will receive right standing with Me, the one who saves them.

Do you want to know what the God-seeker generation looks like? I'll tell you. God-seekers desire to gaze into the face of the God of Abraham, Isaac, and Jacob! The same face that Moses longed to look into.

Listen! An announcement is made: "Lift up your heads, O gates! Be lifted up, O ancient doors! The King of Glory is coming in!" And who is this King of Glory? It's Me, the Lord, strong and mighty! I am the Lord, mighty in battle! You may wonder where I've been. I've been at war! This is a parade of celebration because once again, I'm returning victorious. I rein in My horse beside you as the parade pauses behind Me. I speak to you privately: "It was your battle. The enemy had set an ambush for your destruction. But I defeated the ambush and routed the enemy. Relax now. Enjoy the parade. You're safe." The parade continues while you stare, stunned, dumbfounded, your mouth agape. You were unaware you even had a battle. "Lift up your heads, O gates! Lift them up, O ancient doors, so I can come in from the latest battle on your behalf! I am the Commander of the mighty hosts of heaven! I am the King of Glory!"

The Unfamiliar Psalm

Sometimes I approach a psalm with enthusiasm and great expectation because of my history with God in that particular psalm. Other times, I simply sit down and set my mind to hear from God in a psalm I'm largely unfamiliar with. After probing Psalm 18 with a dear friend one day, I was compelled to ask God the question, "What would it sound like if You spoke this psalm of rescue to me personally?"

Psalm 18 is quite long. I'll process only the first nineteen verses here. But you are certainly invited to explore the entire psalm from the first-person perspective. In this psalm we encounter graphic language of God coming down from heaven to rescue His children.

Once again a picture began to form as I meditated on the psalm. I was facing a particularly difficult period of enemy attack in my life. As I soaked in Psalm 18, I saw myself in an epic battle much like a scene from *Braveheart* or *The Lord of the Rings*. The enemy was everywhere. I controlled my little hill, valiantly swinging my sword against the onslaught of the enemy. Out of the corner of my eye, I could see Jesus flashing a mighty sword, taking out four and five of the enemy with one blow. It was comforting to know we were fighting the same battle.

However, the enemy began to multiply their efforts against me! I could hold off two, maybe three of them. But when the fourth enemy warrior engaged me, I was surrounded by snarls and clashing swords. I fought for all I was worth, but to no avail. It seemed as though I was engulfed by a living, breathing, coiling evil serpent. When I could hardly see a crack of daylight from the snake-like mass entangling me, I screamed,

"Jesus!" Instantly, He was on my little hill. He stepped in front of me, His devastating sword obliterating my foes. He checked to make sure I was okay. Then we both reengaged in the raging battle all around.

Another perspective running parallel to this magnificent illustration of war was that of my cry penetrating the throne room of God. My cries for help were distinct and piercing in heaven. Those angels regularly dispatched to my aid were quivering at the portal of heaven, one eye on me, the other on God where He was seated on His throne. They were saying, "Send me! Please send me! I'll rescue him!" Another would declare even louder, "No! Send me! Send me!" These mighty warring angels were so eager to come to my rescue. Then all of the angels recoiled and gasped, because God Himself stood up. He stepped to the portal and said, "No, I'll go Myself!" Even as I write this memory, my flesh tingles with the power and love of God on behalf of His children. God summoned the mightiest angels and stepped onto their backs. He rode the mighty angels to rescue me!

You've probably heard the expression "When all hell breaks loose." Well, when all heaven breaks loose, it's much, much worse! All heaven broke loose when God came to my rescue.

PSALM 18 IN THE FIRST PERSON

I hear you say, "I love You!" It's music to My ears. I love to hear you say it. I especially love to see you demonstrate your love for Me. I am progressively becoming your strength. You are relying more and more on Me and less on your strength. That's good. Now My power can reside in your weakness!

I am your Rock, your safe place, and your refuge. But I am not only your stationary Rock. I reach out and rescue you. I deliver you and pull you into

My safety. I am the shield that blocks the blows designed to destroy you. I am the horn that sounds, announcing My location and presence so you can simply run toward the sound. I am your stronghold. You call upon me because I am worthy of your praise! When you call upon Me, I respond and save you from your enemies.

I was not unaware . . . I was watching as the cords of death entangled you and began to tie you up and choke you. Your terror mounted, your fear overwhelmed you as the torrents of destruction and ungodliness rained down on you! The cords of the grave were reaching up for you, coiling around you like a living snake. The traps and snares of death were in your face, confronting you, reaching out for you. You couldn't see the light because these aggressive cords of evil had completely wrapped you up in darkness.

Then you cried out to Me for help! In your distress you called out in desperation for deliverance. And I heard you! From the depth of your entangled mess, your cries for help reached My ears. Your scream was heard in My throne room. Then all heaven broke loose! I didn't send My warring angels to your rescue—I came Myself. My response to your cry caused earthquakes—the very foundations of mountains trembled at My anger. Smoke poured from My nostrils, fire shot from My mouth, devouring everything in My path. I threw back the curtain of heaven, and I came down! Dark clouds were under My feet. I mounted the cherubim and rode them. I flew upon the mighty angels. I soared to your rescue on the wings of the wind. I covered Myself with thick darkness. The clouds boiled in advance before Me as the brilliance of My presence pushed them. Hail and bolts of lightning poured from the clouds. I thundered from the heavens. My voice echoed through the skies.

I shot My arrows and scattered your enemies. Great bolts of lightning confused and routed them. When My rebuke was heard, the valleys of the sea were exposed, the foundations of the earth laid bare. Everything was revealed! My fingers wrapped around you securely. I lifted you out of deep waters. I rescued you from your powerful enemy, from those who hated you, from those too mighty for you, from those bent on killing you.

I ended with verse 19. If you choose to write the rest of Psalm 18 in the first person, don't force the following verses to connect with these verses from my rewrite of verses 1-19. This seems to be a major paragraph shift. Enjoy the exercise.

How to Use This Book

Psalms 23, 24, and 18 are deeply personal and touched my soul uniquely as God launched me on this adventure of receiving psalms in the first person. However, while listening to God is never mundane or ordinary, not every psalm exercise is as profound as these. And I have found that returning to a psalm and reengaging God to speak in the first person at a later time results in a whole new experience. The circumstances of my life, the point of my journey with God, and my own emotional and spiritual state come into play, creating an entirely new mystery of hearing God's voice. My prayer is that you can enter into experiences such as these through this book.

Each chapter in *Speak, Lord* is broken into several parts. First, the full text of a psalm is given in a selected translation (various translations are used throughout). Next, we'll briefly explore the main thoughts or theme of this particular psalm before diving into my personal psalm in the first person experience. The rewritten psalm is followed by a Reflection section that captures my thoughts and meditations from writing this psalm in the first person.

The latter part of the chapter helps you personally enter into this experience. The Practice section is broken into Writing Prompts and Devotional Thoughts for you to consider. The writing tips are designed to help you journal this psalm personally in the first person. The thoughts and questions in the Devotional Thoughts are designed to guide you in a devotional experience with this psalm. Each chapter carries the hope of inviting you personally into hearing from God in a fresh and creative approach to the Psalms.

I believe God instructs us through the Psalms to righteously, humbly pour out our hearts to Him in such a way that deeply benefits our souls, our spiritual well-being, and our growth. I count it a privilege and responsibility to learn (from God) how to express myself to Him in ways that actually enhance my relationship with Him. Intimacy has grown significantly in this experiment of receiving psalms in the first person. May God take your pen occasionally as He has at times taken mine, adding powerful words of love, identity, security and significance to the canvas He is painting of you in the Psalms.

My prayer is that you would increasingly enjoy the Psalms— and God Himself. May your relationship with God soar to new heights as you explore the Psalms deeply and vulnerably.

CHAPTER 1

PSALM 1
Who Is Affecting Whom?

Psalm 1

How blessed is the man who does not walk in the counsel
    of the wicked,
Nor stand in the path of sinners,
Nor sit in the seat of scoffers!
But his delight is in the law of the LORD,
And in His law he meditates day and night.
He will be like a tree firmly planted by streams of water,
Which yields its fruit in its season
And its leaf does not wither;
And in whatever he does, he prospers.

The wicked are not so,
But they are like chaff which the wind drives away.
Therefore the wicked will not stand in the judgment,
Nor sinners in the assembly of the righteous.
For the LORD knows the way of the righteous,
But the way of the wicked will perish.

God consistently expresses deep concern about the company we keep. Psalm 1 starts with the phrase "How blessed is the man . . ." *Blessed* can mean "happy, prosperous, fortunate, enviable." This is the kind of life we dream about! But experiencing the blessing of God does not happen accidentally. Blessing comes through the process of making wise and godly choices. God gives us the option of good and bad choices in Psalm 1. Am I impacting the company I keep, or is the company I keep impacting me too severely? Who is affecting whom? Am I a thermostat (setting the tone and temperature in a context of people), or am I a thermometer (simply interpreting the relational temperature and adjusting myself to it)?

Living in God's Word and experiencing the Word living in me is the essential factor not only in making wise choices but in orienting my life increasingly toward the thoughts and purposes God has in regard to this amazing relationship He initiated with me. What will I choose?

Psalm 1 in the First Person

The company you keep is very critical to Me and to your overall success. I really want to bless you. I want you to be happy and prosperous. I want others to look at you and be envious of My goodness evidenced in your life.

I will bless you if you do not walk so close as to hear and consider the counsel of the wicked. Why should you consider their advice?

I will bless you if you do not stop, stand, and lean against the wall where sinners normally travel, down the path they regularly take.

I will bless you if you do not pull up a chair and join the environments where the ungodly scoff and laugh at all that is good and righteous. Don't indulge their crude humor. You become like the company you keep.

The one who avoids these environments, these influences, these people, is the blessed one who finds great delight in what I have written. This blessed one meditates on, soaks in, and marinates in my written Word consistently day and night.

This blessed one will be like a beautiful fruitful tree planted by My clear, nourishing stream of water. They will bear fruit at the proper time. Their leaves will not wither. Whatever they put their hand to I will bless and will cause to prosper.

But not so for the wicked! Not so for those people I told you to avoid! They will blow away like paper in the wind. They will not be able to stand up in the time of judgment. They certainly will not stand in the gathering of My righteous ones, because I know intimately the way of My righteous ones. But the course of the wicked, the ones you are to avoid, is destruction. That's where their counsel will lead you!

Reflections

The first verse shows a progressive engagement with bad company. We can go from bad to worse—from walking, to standing, to sitting! I may choose to walk a path that takes me within the sound of wickedness being discussed. This is not a neighborhood I normally frequent. What's it going to hurt? After all, I'm only catching a few phrases. Tantalized, I consider stopping, perhaps standing in the path they normally travel. Now I'm even more in their company. I'm becoming one of them. Finally, I choose to sit down in the companionship of those who mock and scoff at the values I once held dear. I've become increasingly comfortable with their ungodliness, unrighteousness, and irreverence. This is a slow, subtle movement away from God and into the ways of the world.

"His delight is in the law of the LORD" is perhaps the key phrase that separates these good and bad choices. The word *delight* has often intrigued me. Unless I am a terribly boring person, I must delight in something. I delight in ice cream and popcorn. I delight in mountain climbing and deep relationships. But *delight* as used here has a more powerful, life-course impact. How do I change what I delight in if it is ungodly? Like the tree planted by nourishing water, I must sink my roots deep into God's Word. I must live in God's Word, and His Word must live richly in me. The beautiful end result of such a focus on Scripture is nothing short of life transformation.

When I ask a group of people, "Who has read the Bible from cover to cover?" only a few hands go up. But the practices of reading, hearing, studying, memorizing, and meditating on God's Word are a means to the end of a deeper relationship with God (these are illustrated in the hand illustration; see appendix A). Our attitude toward the Scriptures will have a lot to do with our desire to live in the book that God wrote. How we view the Bible—whether strictly as God's laws to be obeyed (which is true, but limited), or as God's letter of invitation to an ultimate, mind-blowing relationship—will determine our motivation to focus our delight, our pleasure, our thrill on hearing from God in His living and active Word (Hebrews 4:12). This is what God intends when He says, "His delight is in the law of the LORD."

Oftentimes we allow the culture of our day to determine how we relate to God and His Word. We live in a sound-bite age. We want only a little bit at a time. Our attention span will not tolerate larger portions. But as followers of the only true living God, we could choose to allow God and His Word to determine our level of devotion and adjustment to His written

4

Word. I hope we will not view "delighting in the law of the LORD" as something beyond our grasp.

Practice

Writing Prompts

» Always begin by reviewing the question, "Lord, what would it sound like if You spoke this psalm to me personally?"

» Consider verse 1. Read it in several translations until you gain a good sense of God's heart being expressed. Notice that God starts with those who are not blessed. Try your hand at writing this first verse as though God were speaking it to you personally. Allow me to offer a suggested beginning. Remember, this is God speaking: "I fully intend to bless the person who . . ." Now complete the sentence as you hear God answer the question.

» Reflect on verse 2. Altering the phrase "the law of the LORD" to say "My law" begins to shift the verse into first person. You may prefer the phrase, "My proven instructions for living . . ." The next phrase, "in His law he meditates," could sound like, "in My instructions for successful living, you meditate." So verse 2, spoken from God's point of view, might look something like this: "But your delight is in My proven instructions for living, and in My instructions for successful living you meditate day and night."

» With a little flair from alternate translations and possible meditation, you may come up with something like this for verse

2: "But in contrast, your sheer joy and deep hunger is for My Word, and in My Word you chew and digest truth, and you are set free day and night." Here, *delight* is expanded into "sheer joy and deep hunger." The complex word *meditate* is opened to express "chew" (a literal definition for *meditate*) and "digest" (what happens after you chew and swallow?), and "truth" is substituted for *God's Word*. From John 8:32, drawing from our possible past experience in God's Word, the phrase "the truth will set you free" can easily be added to further understand the results of this delight in God's Word. Hopefully you begin to see the value of living in God's Word and God's Word living in you.

» Enjoy rewriting the rest of this psalm in the first person!

Devotional Thoughts

» How might God be extending an invitation to you for deeper relationship through verses 1 and 2? What would His invitation sound like?

» Observe the progression of commitment to evil through the words *walk*, *stand*, and *sit*. How would you expand and embellish this growing engagement with evil in your own words?

» Be vulnerable with the Lord. Where are you in any level of commitment to entertaining the world and its ways that are alien to God and His ways?

» "He will be like the tree . . ." gives us a nice on-ramp for thinking like a tree. Consider the perspective of the tree—*firmly planted*, etc. What is it like to have such a rich environment for growth and development to become all you were intended to be?

CHAPTER 2

PSALM 2
The Nations Versus God

Psalm 2 (NIV)

Why do the nations conspire
    and the peoples plot in vain?
The kings of the earth rise up
    and the rulers band together
    against the LORD and against his anointed, saying,
"Let us break their chains
    and throw off their shackles."

The One enthroned in heaven laughs;
    the Lord scoffs at them.
He rebukes them in his anger
    and terrifies them in his wrath, saying,
"I have installed my king
    on Zion, my holy mountain."

I will proclaim the LORD's decree:

He said to me, "You are my son;
    today I have become your father.
Ask me,
    and I will make the nations your inheritance,
    the ends of the earth your possession.
You will break them with a rod of iron;
    you will dash them to pieces like pottery."

Therefore, you kings, be wise;
    be warned, you rulers of the earth.
Serve the LORD with fear
    and celebrate his rule with trembling.
Kiss his son, or he will be angry
    and your way will lead to your destruction,
for his wrath can flare up in a moment.
    Blessed are all who take refuge in him.

Tiny, insignificant nations proudly puff out their chests, flexing their muscles against the God of heaven. Dictators and rulers strut around proclaiming that they will not submit to this God or any god. How absurd! God tolerates them for a season—and then He rebukes them to do homage to His installed King, His own Son. One day these rulers of the earth will be profoundly surprised and shocked to realize who they were opposing.

Psalm 2 in the First Person

Listen to them! They're in an uproar! They plot together, egging one another on, provoking shouts and taunts from still other nations. They devise an empty and fruitless plan. The rulers of the world collaborate and give counsel to one another against Me. They think that if they get everyone on their side, they can actually come against Me and My Anointed One. Can you believe it? They want to throw off all restraints that might be associated with bending their knee to Me. They are like tiny puffed-up buffoons raging against the very One who created them. Watch out, little nations. You might get stepped on!

I sit on My throne in heaven and laugh. I mock their tirades and scoff at their declarations of independence. The very idea of mere mortal man taking a stand against Me! For crying out loud, I'm God! I speak to them out of the anger they arouse in Me. When they hear My fury they will recoil in terror! They have no idea who they are messing with. They have no idea who they are insulting.

But the true and secure reality is this: I have enthroned and installed My King on My holy mountain, Zion. He will tell of My announcements of truth and righteousness. I declared to Him, "You are My Son! Today I have begotten You. Ask Me, dare to ask Me, and these very nations that are in an uproar I will give to You as Your inheritance. I will give the very ends of the earth as Your personal possession. You will break them with Your rod of iron. You will smash them like pottery!"

Now listen to Me, you kings of the earth, you mere mortals—show some humility and respect! Be warned, you judges and leaders of the world. Bow down and worship the only true God with fear and awe. Rejoice even as you tremble at Him. Kiss His hand in honor. Do homage to My Son. He could so easily destroy you with a word due to the anger you provoke. You could perish and no one would care. His wrath may suddenly be kindled. But My blessed ones hide in Him!

Reflections

My younger cousin once said to his parents, "When I get big and you get little, you're going to really be sorry." Sounds like mere created men conspiring against the Creator: "If enough of us get together, we can throw off these restrictions and live the way we want to live. We can be God ourselves!" Absurd. Preposterous. Were it not for the seriousness of the challenge of nations against God, one would be prone to laugh along with God at the ludicrousness of this scenario. The tower of Babel didn't work. But we still try!

It's easy to point the finger and laugh at nonsensical nations who conspire to free themselves of God and His restraints. But it's just as easy to overlook how we do the same thing in our own hearts as we live our lives the way that pleases us most. There is a God, and none of us are Him.

I'm reminded of a conversation between a woman and her son, who was a relatively young believer transitioning from college to the work world. They were discussing his need to pray about his career decision. What would he do with his life?

"Why do I need to pray?" he asked her. "It's *my* life! I'll do what I want with it!"

Once again, it's easy to chuckle at the severe immaturity of such a statement. But this young man actually had the guts to express openly what most of us really believe on the inside.

It's sobering and at times terrifying to consider how I (and certainly nations) spit in God's face with declarations of independent living. Each of us who follow Christ has been "bought with a price," the very blood of Jesus—"therefore glorify God in my body!" (1 Corinthians 6:20). The greater reality is that we "belong" to God. We have been purchased with the highest price ever paid, the life-blood of Jesus! So we shouldn't ask, "What should I do with *my* life? What is God's will for *my* life?" A more biblically saturated question might be, "What does God want to do with the life He bought?" In other words, this life is not mine any longer.

God is remarkably kind and forgiving as I sort through life, "deciding" where I will pay homage. Will I pay tribute to the only true living God, or will I resolve to be my own god once again? Until I see Him face-to-face, I have the beautiful choice to honor and worship the Son, the King God Himself has installed. I choose to worship Him from my deepest heart, not waiting to be compelled by His returning.

O rulers of earth—choose wisely.

Practice

Writing Prompts

» Probe verses 1-3, transferring the outrageous disrespect of a five-year-old against his or her parents to this context of nations rebelling against God. The child is deadly serious in their defiance to run away and start a new life. Yet the extent of the rebellion only gets the child into the backyard, spending the night in a tent! Try this: "These nations sound like undisciplined, arrogant children. They are full of themselves! I will tolerate their insubordination for only so long. Watch your step, smart-mouthed sassers! You don't know Whom you are talking to! You want to throw off all restraints. But you don't even know that those restraints are there for your good."

» Now in verses 4-6, allow yourself to enter into the anger of God at such a disrespectful barrage (not against a five-year-old, but against rebellious adults). Pause and meditate on the Lord's emotions when faced with His creation denying His very existence. Here is a beginning phrase to get you started: "Your insolence has caused Me to rise up from My throne! The angels around Me gasped as they overheard your rude tirade."

» God shifts focus to His beloved Son in verses 7-9, then He shifts back to the rebellious nations for His final lecture of correction. Try to represent the Father's deep pleasure with His Son in this context.

» Enjoy rewriting the rest of this psalm in the first person!

Devotional Thoughts

» Have you ever raged against God like these ungodly nations? I've had people tell me they even swear when they speak to God. I cringe on the inside when I hear them. But then I think, *God can handle His unruly children just fine.* God isn't shaken. But is there truly a benefit for human beings in this disrespectful approach? Reflect on times when you have brought hot emotions to God. As you consider the entirety of the Psalms, do you desire to alter your approach? Could there be a more humble attitude that would contribute to your eventual transformation?

» Would you consider renewing your commitment to live as though you belong to God? To live in the knowledge that your life is actually His and that He alone is God and can do whatever He desires with your life?

CHAPTER 3

PSALM 3

A Shield Around Me

Psalm 3 (MSG)

GOD! Look! Enemies past counting!
Enemies sprouting like mushrooms,
Mobs of them all around me, roaring their mockery:
"Hah! No help for *him* from God!"

But you, GOD, shield me on all sides;
You ground my feet, you lift my head high;
With all my might I shout up to GOD,
His answers thunder from the holy mountain.

I stretch myself out. I sleep.
Then I'm up again—rested, tall and steady,
Fearless before the enemy mobs
Coming at me from all sides.

Up, GOD! My God, help me!
Slap their faces,
First this cheek, then the other,
Your fist hard in their teeth!

Real help comes from GOD.
Your blessing clothes your people!

What a gut-wrenching scenario! David's own son Absalom rose up against his father to take the throne. The story is found in 2 Samuel 15–18. Absalom connived and conspired to turn the people against his father. David could have crushed the uprising with his seasoned warriors. But he removed himself and his family from the royal city, trusting God with the outcome. This psalm captures some of the passion and agony of David in the clutches of this rebellion.

Psalm 3 in the First Person

I hear you cry out to Me! I can see that your enemies are increasing in number. Those you thought were with you are turning against you. I hear them mocking you. They are even mocking Me. They are saying, "God will not deliver you this time. There is no help for you from God or anyone else!" Pause, and calmly think of that.

I'm so proud of you. You know Me well! Even when your enemies surround you and outnumber you, even when your so-called friends take up arms against you, you say with confidence that Jehovah is your Shield. I am your glory. I am the One who lifts your downturned head. I surround you with My presence. I stand between you and your enemies. I heard your cry from My holy mountain, and I answered you. Pause, and calmly think of that.

You lay down and sleep like a baby. You awake without fear because I am the One watching over you. Even if thousands come against you, even tens of thousands, you will not be afraid. Even if they establish themselves against you in battle formation, you do not fear.

Again you call to Me to save you. I rise up! I hover over your enemies. I strike them in the face. I break their teeth. They know they have been punched by the Mighty One! Ultimate help and rescue comes from Me. My blessing is upon all My people. Pause, and calmly think of that.

Reflections

This psalm invited me into the heart and agony of David as a father. In the face of an army being formed right under his nose, the mighty warrior of God chose not to squelch his enemies, his brothers, his own son. This was civil war—not only within the nation of God, but within David's immediate family. How do you deal with your own son in light of such severe rebellion? David had no fight left in him. He walked away with his head down in shame. How had he failed so miserably as a father? Was God removing him from leadership? God Himself would be the judge of his future as king. Despite everything, he clung to his passionate relationship with God. God was his shield and protector. David's faith was tested in this crucible of mutiny. He walked away from his kingdom. But he did not walk away from his God.

Practice

Writing Prompts

» Read 2 Samuel 15–18 to gain perspective on this particular psalm.

» Consider in verse 1 that David's focused attention is on his adversaries. From this point of view, here are some beginning phrases: "I hear your cries in My throne room. But your perspective is skewed. Take your eyes off your enemies for a moment and . . ."

» In verse 3, David's attention adjusts back to God Himself. Now, looking into the face of God, your psalm in the first person might express, "I am a shield all around you. You are much safer than you were aware. I put your feet on solid ground. I lift your head . . ."

» Enjoy rewriting the rest of this psalm in the first person!

Devotional Thoughts

» Imagine your son, your own flesh and blood, turning against you in open revolt. You could easily destroy this uprising. Chances are your most mighty warriors are still with you. But perhaps this rebellion is from God. Perhaps God has determined that your days as leader are over. You decide to walk away, trusting that if God wants you to lead, then nothing will come of this uprising. And not only do you walk away, but you are shamed and ridiculed as you retreat. Allow your heart to enter into this grueling episode. Can you trust God with your reputation, with your honor, in the face of scorn and mockery?

» Are your enemies increasing? Your enemies are probably not those who would threaten your life. Perhaps they are those who simply oppose you, those who make life more difficult and miserable than necessary. Are your eyes on your enemies, or are your eyes on God? It's so easy to lose perspective on God when enemies are in our faces, taunting us, ridiculing us. Do you need to adjust your perspective from enemy focus to God focus? Ephesians 2:6 says He "raised us up with Him, and seated us with Him in the heavenly places." That's past tense—a done deal! Our genuine perspective can be from the throne room of our Father, looking down on our earthly enemies and struggles from the lap of God. Do you need a perspective adjustment?

» Do you believe the mocking chant, "There is no delivery for him [or her] from God?" Do you really believe that God has turned His back on you? Others would have you believe this lie. But what does God say? In the face of your worst nightmare, what do you believe about the promised ongoing presence of your God?

» Do you sleep well? Or do you experience fitful, fearful sleep? God has better rest for His beloved. Psalm 4:8 says, "In peace I will both lie down and sleep, for You alone, O LORD, make me to dwell in safety." Once again, God's promised, abiding presence is always our reality, even though all of hell would have us believe differently. What will you believe? And how do you believe something new? How do you actually exchange one belief, discovered to be a lie, for the truth? Certainly it is a process! But I see in David's life a genuine trust and deep reliance on God, and I express to my Father, "I see what David has. I don't have it. But I want it. Will you build this beautiful intimacy into our Father-son relationship?" When my precious children or grandchildren reveal the longing of their hearts to me, especially when they genuinely want more of me, they know I will move heaven and earth to provide all I can for them. How much more will our heavenly Father overwhelmingly extend Himself to us as children? Tell your heavenly Father you want some of that peaceful sleep. Trust Him to lead you in a new belief and process of safe sleep.

CHAPTER 4

PSALM 19
Creation Speaks of God

Psalm 19 (ESV)

The heavens declare the glory of God,
    and the sky above proclaims his handiwork.
Day to day pours out speech,
    and night to night reveals knowledge.
There is no speech, nor are there words,
    whose voice is not heard.
Their voice goes out through all the earth,
    and their words to the end of the world.
In them he has set a tent for the sun,
    which comes out like a bridegroom leaving
        his chamber,
and, like a strong man, runs its course with joy.
Its rising is from the end of the heavens,
    and its circuit to the end of them,
    and there is nothing hidden from its heat.

The law of the LORD is perfect,
    reviving the soul;
the testimony of the LORD is sure,
    making wise the simple;
the precepts of the LORD are right,
    rejoicing the heart;
the commandment of the LORD is pure,
    enlightening the eyes;
the fear of the LORD is clean,
    enduring forever;
the rules of the LORD are true,
    and righteous altogether.
More to be desired are they than gold,
    even much fine gold;
sweeter also than honey
    and drippings of the honeycomb.
Moreover, by them is your servant warned;
    in keeping them there is great reward.

Who can discern his errors?
    Declare me innocent from hidden faults.
Keep back your servant also from
      presumptuous sins;
    let them not have dominion over me!
Then I shall be blameless,
    and innocent of great transgression.
Let the words of my mouth and the meditation
    of my heart
    be acceptable in your sight,
    O LORD, my rock and my redeemer.

As you examine psalms from the first person, a few psalms will present more of a challenge, requiring extended meditation and examination. Psalm 19 was a difficult psalm for me to process in the first person. Who was speaking? To whom were they speaking? But when the light broke through my dim view, Psalm 19 became one of my favorites! All of creation is speaking on a daily basis of the glory, power, wonder, and magnificence of God. Day speaks to night. Night speaks to day. Both declare the magnificent spectacle they have the privilege of observing as God reveals Himself. Listen to what they have to say!

Psalm 19 in the First Person

Shhhh! Listen. Do you hear it? Listen carefully. Focus. Heaven is speaking, telling of My glory. The expanse of boundless heaven is declaring what is seen of the works of My hands. And not only does heaven speak, but day announces to the following day, saying, "You won't believe what I saw of God just now!" Each day pours forth speech. And in the silence and stillness of night, whispers reveal more knowledge grasped of Me. What day has seen and heard is joyfully passed on to night. Night discusses these revelations till the following morning. Then as dawn approaches, fresh thoughts are passed on as day begins again. There is no speech. There are no words. Voices are not heard. Yet mysteriously, phrases permeate earth. Listen carefully and you'll hear their sounds, utterances to the ends of the earth.

Sunrise is a marriage celebration! The strong husband exits his tent, his passions deeply satisfied with the bride of his dreams.

Sunrise! My name, God Most High, is announced with brilliant expressions and revelations never seen before as the red orange fireball bursts forth from his tent! He races across the heavens, shouting knowledge and

SPEAK, LORD

understanding until he approaches evening. He prepares to hand off to night, breathlessly recounting all he saw and heard of God's glory in his tour of light.

Sunset! Painted across the sky with My finger, enlightening, illuminating all who would listen and observe. The kiss of day with night, creating anticipation of Me in the darkness. If you would listen, recognize that I am so much more than you have ever imagined.

Unspoken yet perceptible expressions of My glory rise up to heaven, run a circuit to the far corners of heaven, exposing the heavenly expanse. All creation speaks of My presence.

And My living and active Word speaks too. My law is perfection, restoring your soul. My testimony is sure, trustworthy, reliable, making even the simple wise. My precepts are right, accurate, on target, causing your heart to rejoice. My commandment is pure, refined, unblemished, opening and enlightening your eyes. Fearing Me makes you clean, an everlasting purification. My judgments are true, no lying, completely righteous. All of these gifts and expressions of Me, My law, My testimony, My precepts, My commandments, fear of Me, and My judgments, are more desirable than gold, even refined, highest-carat gold. They are sweeter than honey, the best drippings from the honeycomb. By these words, sounds, revelations, and expressions of Me, you, precious one, are warned. And in adjusting your life to them, you will find great reward.

Reflections

I love this snippet by Elizabeth Barrett Browning: "Earth's crammed with heaven, and every common bush afire with God, but only he who sees takes off his shoes; the rest sit round and pluck blackberries."

She captures the heart and mind-set we must have if we are

to hear day and night express what they learned of God in their brief timespan.

Personifying day and night helped make this psalm come alive. Both day and night are experiencing God in beautiful new, exciting ways, recording and passing on to the next in line all that they see, learn, and taste of God.

Sun bursts forth, taking the baton from night, hearing dawn's report of new revelations from God during the darkness. Then sun races through the day with his own gathering of the freshness of God's instruction. It's rich to allow my sanctified imagination, focused on God Himself, to run with these word pictures. I feel so much closer to God throughout a normal day as I pause to observe every element of creation voicing unique perspectives about God and His handiwork of the day.

Next comes the detailed proclamation about God via His own words incarnate in our language! It doesn't get any better than this! Until, of course, we see Him face-to-face and finally see the fullness of His person, His glory, His holiness, His love.

Love God's Word. Receive His embrace reaching out for you from His spoken, recorded message. Gold, silver, diamonds, rubies, and emeralds are nothing but trinkets when compared to the supreme value and worth of God's precious, priceless Word.

Practice

Writing Prompts

» Ponder verses 1-4, with the elements of nature taking on unique personalities and voices. What would it sound like if heaven and earth, day and night spoke of the revelation of God during their tenure? Consider this beginning: "Heaven is eager to express My glory . . ." Allow your imagination to soar with the heart of nature, declaring the beauty, majesty, and magnificence of God on display.

» Verses 4-6 show the bridegroom sun bursting forth with His announcement of God's glory. How would you capture such a joyous speech from the eager groom? Perhaps, "Bridegroom Fireball is eager to speak of My glory experienced during his circuit across the heavens. His dawn kisses earth good morning. His sunset snuggles her good night."

» Verses 7-11 shift to the revelation of God found in unique aspects of Scripture. Contemplate the difference between law and testimony, precept and commandment. Would other translations help you unpack these particular aspects of God's written Word?

» How might God express His heart for you in verses 12-14 as He speaks to the way you live? Perhaps something like, "I know you better than you know yourself. And I know how difficult it is for you to avoid sin. Remember, all nature is announcing My glory as you struggle to live according to My wishes. Help is available all around you. The key is to focus on Me, following in the footsteps of heaven and earth, day and night."

» Enjoy rewriting the rest of this psalm in the first person!

Devotional Thoughts

» Take some time to pause and quietly observe a sunrise, glory in a sunset. Can you imagine what night might say to day? Listen for day to announce to evening with excitement the visions of God's glory splashed across the sky. Practice the historical disciplines of silence and solitude as you listen carefully for God to reveal His glory.

» Reflect on your personal belief regarding the high value assigned to God's written Word in this psalm. Meditate on phrases from Psalm 119 as you contemplate expanding your conviction of what you believe about Scripture.

CHAPTER 5

PSALM 25
No Shame

Psalm 25

To You, O LORD, I lift up my soul.
O my God, in You I trust,
Do not let me be ashamed;
Do not let my enemies exult over me.
Indeed, none of those who wait for You will be ashamed;
Those who deal treacherously without cause
      will be ashamed.

Make me know Your ways, O LORD;
Teach me Your paths.
Lead me in Your truth and teach me,
For You are the God of my salvation;
For You I wait all the day.
Remember, O LORD, Your compassion and
      Your lovingkindnesses,
For they have been from of old.

Do not remember the sins of my youth or
      my transgressions;
According to Your lovingkindness remember me,
For Your goodness' sake, O LORD.
Good and upright is the LORD;
Therefore He instructs sinners in the way.
He leads the humble in justice,
And He teaches the humble His way.
All the paths of the LORD are lovingkindness and truth
To those who keep His covenant and His testimonies.
For Your name's sake, O LORD,
Pardon my iniquity, for it is great.

Who is the man who fears the LORD?
He will instruct him in the way he should choose.
His soul will abide in prosperity,
And his descendants will inherit the land.
The secret of the LORD is for those who fear Him,
And He will make them know His covenant.
My eyes are continually toward the LORD,
For He will pluck my feet out of the net.

Turn to me and be gracious to me,
For I am lonely and afflicted.
The troubles of my heart are enlarged;
Bring me out of my distresses.
Look upon my affliction and my trouble,
And forgive all my sins.
Look upon my enemies, for they are many,
And they hate me with violent hatred.

Guard my soul and deliver me;
Do not let me be ashamed, for I take refuge in You.
Let integrity and uprightness preserve me,
For I wait for You.
Redeem Israel, O God,
Out of all his troubles.

This is a powerful, healing rescue psalm, one where God takes the pen and weaves our story into the life of the psalmist. The world and everything in it is potentially a source of red-faced shame for us. But not so with our God! He will not let us be put to shame, and He will shame those who would shame us.

Psalm 25 in the First Person

Lift up your soul to Me! Don't be afraid. Soar with Me. Fly with Me! I am your God, the Lover of your soul. In Me alone you can trust. I will not let you be shamed. Humiliation and embarrassment are not for My children. I will not allow your enemies to celebrate your defeat. None who wait for Me will be ashamed. But those who are cruel and deceitful will be put to shame.

I will help you know My ways. Wait eagerly for Me. Wait on tiptoes for Me! I will instruct you in My chosen paths. I will lead you in My truth and I will teach you, because I am God, the one and only God of your salvation. My hand will reassure you. My smile will motivate you.

Wait with anticipation for Me, even if you must wait all day! Don't worry—I will remember My compassion and love mixed, mingled with My kindness. Those qualities you like so much about Me are quite ancient and plentiful. My compassion and lovingkindness have always been with Me. Your youthful indulgences are tempting you. Yet your sins are quickly forgotten by Me. When I wash your blemishes with My blood, no spots are left, no remnants remind Me of your sin. The sins you can't seem to forget, I don't recall! I remember you according to My lovingkindness, not according to your sin. My goodness washes over you like a warm bath. I am good and I am upright—nothing less. I am the only One who can guide sinners out of their tangled mess. I lead the humble, afflicted ones into My courtroom for justice. I teach them My way. All of My pathways are lovingkindness and truth for those who are covenant keepers with Me. For the sake of My great name, Yahweh, Jehovah, I will pardon your sin, no matter how great, no matter how foolish! After all, you are My child.

Do you fear Me? Do you tremble in My presence? Stand in awe before Me! Allow My presence to have its profound impact upon you. If you do so, I will instruct you in the best choice for your next chapter. Your soul will abide in prosperity, in My goodness. Your children will inherit the land. Do you fear Me? My secret counsel is for those who fear Me. Those are the ones I will share privately with. I will pull them close and whisper My secrets in their ear. I will reveal to them My covenant. Are your eyes continually toward Me? Look at Me. I will snatch your feet out of the net. Yes, you were caught. But once again, I came to your rescue. I am so ready to turn to you and be gracious to you. Just cry out to Me! Can you humble yourself and do that? Or must you continue trying to save yourself? I know you are lonely and afflicted. I know the troubles of your heart grow and multiply. But I will bring you out of your distress. I see your affliction and trouble, your toil. I am right here, ready to forgive all of your sins. Every one of them! No sin is too great! Will you let Me into the dark closet of your heart? You think these pampered sins are hidden from Me, but their offensive smell is unavoidable. Only I can purge those deep blemishes from your soul. Will you trust Me?

I also see your enemies. You have a lot of adversaries. Your foes hate you with a hot, vicious hatred. They have no idea that I am the Guardian of your soul. I deliver you. I protect you. Take refuge in Me! Run to Me!

Don't attempt to fight this battle on your own. I will not let you be shamed. I took your shame to the cross. I despised the shame for you. I shamed not only your shame but the very source of your shame, that wicked Shamer! I won the ultimate victory! I destroyed the Shamer with the exact shame he intended to inflict on you. The result? No more shame. Now My integrity and uprightness preserve you. Wait for Me. Wait with anticipation. Don't move ahead without Me. Always wait for Me. Watch eagerly for My rescue operation. I will ransom you out of all your troubles. I will do the same for all My people.

Reflections

Where do I look for my source of life? Do I have expectant hope that if I wait eagerly for God, He will not let me down? If I look to anything else or anyone else for life, being ashamed is inevitable. Not so in God's kingdom!

I love the picture of eagerly waiting on tiptoes, like a child who knows Grandpa is coming. I'll never forget the sheer joy of my two-year-old granddaughter watching out the window for my promised arrival. She burst from the front door, ran helter-skelter down the sidewalk, and literally jumped into my waiting arms. What innocent, reckless, and abandoned joy and trust! And what joy burst forth from my own heart in this wild expression of pleasure and delight. That's the picture of waiting on God here. Could I have such an effect upon the heart of God? Would He receive such unbounded joy at my leaping into His arms?

Yet shame kicks in so easily, so quickly, so naturally. When I sin, I'm ashamed to have done the same thing again. I think, *If I were God, I wouldn't want to forgive me! He must be sick and tired of me coming again and again with my head hung low.* Yet our God is like the father of the Prodigal Son. The son didn't even get to finish his rehearsed speech when he came dragging his sin home (Luke 15). His dad ran to greet him, gave him the best robe, the signet ring for his finger, new sandals for his feet! He threw a big party to celebrate the return, the repentance of his wandering son. That's how my Father is eager to receive me back from "one more time" down the nasty, disgusting road I'm prone to choose.

Then my Father pulls me in so close I can smell His aftershave. He tells me the secrets of His heart. Only the privileged get to hear these secrets! And often His secrets are hard-to-believe, life-changing thoughts regarding me—but His heart is full of them. Oh, may His truth set me free to actually become the kind of person who would live freed from shame.

It's comforting to realize my God knows how hard life is. He knows my lonely, vulnerable spirals that suck me into old destructive patterns. He is not just ready to receive me back— He never left! He actually went through the sin path with me! He wept while I indulged my flesh, my ego, my broken places.

But the lying Shamer is bent on my destruction. He floods my ear with how unlovable, how disgusting, how revolting I really am. Who do I think I am to escape my repulsive past? His giant sword called Shame is drawn against me once again. My battered, pathetic shield rises, trembling, anticipating my demise. But the knockout never comes! A mighty warrior sweeps me behind His back with His powerful arm. Jesus, Captain of the Lord's host, takes the sword out of the Shamer's powerful fist and turns it on my Enemy. The Shamer is destroyed with the cross of Jesus. Then Jesus turns to me with a big smile—I am His joy.

This is a powerful, life-altering story from my journey. The Enemy used the shameful truth about me to slowly, methodically destroy me and everything I loved. Then God unfolded the truth of Hebrews 12:2: "Fixing our eyes on Jesus, the author and perfecter of faith, who for the joy set before Him endured the cross, despising the shame, and has sat down at the right hand of the throne of God." Why were Jesus and the Father willing to pay such a terrible price with the Cross? I believe it's because they wanted me back! They wanted you back! And once they accomplished our rescues, we are the source of their joy!

Practice

Writing Prompts

» As you ask the question, "Lord, what would it sound like if You spoke this psalm to me personally?" envision yourself seated with God in heaven (Ephesians 2:6). Now listen to the Lord rearrange the words of this first sentence to originate with Him. Consider a beginning phrase such as, "Your eyes are up. Your arms are up. Your face is up. Your soul is lifted up to Me. Trust Me."

» Shame is a very defeating force against us, a favorite weapon of our Enemy. We live in a world of shame. Being careful to not pull your own negative thoughts about yourself into this rewrite, listen to God speak of your shame from His perspective. Remember, He destroyed shame with the Cross (Hebrews 12:2). Perhaps His thoughts could be, "Shame does not come from Me. I am the source of life, goodness, mercy, and love. Does that sound like shame to you? Let Me be different from your world. Let Me be different from anything you have ever imagined."

» Enjoy journaling the rest of this psalm in the first person.

Devotional Thoughts

» Where is your soul lifted up? What (or who) is the source you look to for life? If your source of life is not God alone, shame and the Shamer have a death grip on you. You may want to turn to Psalm 51 and find release from the grip of shame through true repentance.

» Meditate on God's compassion and love mingled with kindness. Ask God to wash you in the warm bath of His goodness. Is it hard for you to believe that God feels this way about you? He can only love you to the extent you allow Him to love you, regardless of the vastness of His love for you. Will you let Him love you? Receive His love. Put your arms down, stop resisting, and receive His embrace.

» God is not your enemy. But you do have an Enemy. Are you so confused you can't tell who your real enemy is? The father of lies would have you believe that God is your enemy. He would have you believe that God is the source of your shame. Remember, your enemy is the father of lies.

» Allow the freedom-from-shame words from Psalm 25 to set you free from the humiliation, embarrassment, and shame the Shamer has been pounding you with. Perhaps your soul is so downcast that you dare not lift your face to your Father. Read Psalm 25 over and over again. Allow God's words to wash over you, cleansing you of shame's oppression.

» Is there a sword named Shame being wielded against your battered shield of faith? Meditate on the picture revealed from Hebrews 12:2 of the mighty warrior, Jesus, stepping into your battle to fight for you. You could also meditate on Colossians 2:8-15 and Hebrews 9:11-14.

» Now write your own story. Create your own picture of God's mighty rescue from the sword of Shame that has been plaguing you.

CHAPTER 6

PSALM 27
Whom Shall I Fear?

Psalm 27 (AMP)

The Lord is my Light and my Salvation—whom shall I fear
or dread? The Lord is the Refuge and Stronghold of
my life—of whom shall I be afraid?
When the wicked, even my enemies and my foes, came
upon me to eat up my flesh, they stumbled and fell.
Though a host encamp against me, my heart shall not fear;
though war arise against me, [even then] in this will
I be confident.
One thing have I asked of the Lord, that will I seek, inquire
for, and [insistently] require: that I may dwell in
the house of the Lord [in His presence] all the days
of my life, to behold and gaze upon the beauty [the
sweet attractiveness and the delightful loveliness]
of the Lord and to meditate, consider, and inquire
in His temple.

For in the day of trouble He will hide me in His shelter; in
the secret place of His tent will He hide me; He will
set me high upon a rock.

And now shall my head be lifted up above my enemies
round about me; in His tent I will offer sacrifices
and shouting of joy; I will sing, yes, I will sing
praises to the Lord.

Hear, O Lord, when I cry aloud; have mercy and be gracious
to me and answer me!

You have said, Seek My face [inquire for and require My
presence as your vital need]. My heart says to You,
Your face (Your presence), Lord, will I seek, inquire
for, and require [of necessity and on the authority of
Your Word].

Hide not Your face from me; turn not Your servant
away in anger, You Who have been my help!
Cast me not off, neither forsake me, O God of
my salvation!

Although my father and my mother have forsaken
me, yet the Lord will take me up [adopt me
as His child].

Teach me Your way, O Lord, and lead me in a plain and
even path because of my enemies [those who lie
in wait for me].

Give me not up to the will of my adversaries, for false
witnesses have risen up against me; they breathe
out cruelty and violence.

[What, what would have become of me] had I not believed
that I would see the Lord's goodness in the land of
the living!

Wait and hope for and expect the Lord; be brave and
of good courage and let your heart be stout and
enduring. Yes, wait for and hope for and expect
the Lord.

In this psalm, David exudes confident, even boastful assurance
that God is on his side. In the face of a horde of enemies with
an arsenal of schemes all designed to wreak havoc on his life,
David's faith and trust in God reveal a solid, secure foundation
of relationship: "One thing, only one thing do I really desire.
That one thing I will seek after passionately. To dwell, to live,
to set up house in God's house for the rest of my life. To gaze
upon His beauty, to be captivated, mesmerized by His presence. And in that privileged place, to inquire of the Lord." These
words seem to be the backbone of David's strong conviction
in the Lord's intervention. But even though David had this
"one desire," he couldn't fulfill it because of the locale of the
temple of God. Yet we have the temple of God residing in us
(1 Corinthians 3:16; 6:19-20), but we often waver significantly
in having this "one desire." One of those conundrums in life.
How much more intimate, desirous, and authentic my relationship with God would be if my many desires were refined to this
one desire.

Psalm 27 in the First Person

*I am Jehovah, the One who fights for you. I deliver you. I save you from your
vicious enemies. I shine and you can see. I rescue and you are safe. Fear no
one. Fear nothing. What would you compare to Me that is worthy of fear?*

Watch when those evil marauders attack you and everything you love.

With teeth bared, they seek your flesh. Yet mysteriously they stumble and fall on their faces!

A mighty army may encamp against you, but still you know of My victorious history. Put your heart at ease. Don't fear. Even though war cries are heard outside your gates, conflict imminent, and despite pending battle, put your confidence in Me.

I hear your solitary heart cry. You do not lust for many things. You are hungering for Me! And I will satisfy your longing. I will meet your deepest need. I'm pleased that you want to move into My house. I want to fill your meditations with deeper relationship with Me. Gaze into My face, experience the beauty of My presence.

Troublesome days will come. When danger arrives, practiced familiarity with My dwelling place gives you confidence to hide in My secret place. I will lift you up to My highest rock ledge, secure from harm.

Now your head is far above, exalted over your enemies. They surround you but cannot get to you. With the backdrop of their war cries, your worship of Me is especially sweet. Your living sacrifice satisfies My soul; it is your ultimate gift to Me.

I hear when you cry out. I'm always attentive to your voice. My mercy is on its way. My grace is poised to be poured out.

I said to you, "Seek My face!" Your heart responded in My presence, "Your face, O God, I will seek!"

Even though you have known Me tenderly, still you fear My face turning away. You fear My rejection. I will not abandon you. Quite the contrary— I am your deliverer! I rescue! I break chains! I open prison doors!

Perhaps your father and mother could come to the end of their rope and abandon you. Even if they could reject you, never, never, never will I abandon you. Not only that, I will search for you when you have been abandoned.

My ways are much more subtle than doing the right thing. It's doing the right thing the right way. My way. For this you must spend extended time with Me, watching how I work, how I live. Follow Me in what is often the obscure path. It is the little-known path, My way around the ambush set by your foes.

Your antagonists have stacked the deck against you. Liars are willing to testify falsely against you. They lie in wait, passionately desiring to destroy you, bit by bit. They think they have you. But I will never deliver you over to their twisted schemes.

I can read your inner reflections like a book. You are wondering, musing, what your life would be like if you had no hope, no expectation that in the midst of chaos and despair, you would live to see My goodness. Your strong belief, your true knowledge and experience of Me pulls you through again.

Focus on Me. Wait for Me. Hope in Me. Rely on Me. I will not let you down. Find your strength in Me. Allow your confidence to grow because you genuinely know Me. I'll say it again because it's your lifeline: wait for Me.

Reflections

In verses 1-3, David appears to have had reason to fear: evildoers, adversaries, and even an army are amassed against him. But David also had an enviable relationship with God: God said he was "a man after my own heart; he will do everything I want him to do" (Acts 13:22, NIV). The Psalms expose unusual, zealous, heart-to-heart, soul-to-soul connection between God and His poet. Whether we believe that the door is open to us just as it was to David will determine our pursuit of increasing relationship with God.

God said to David, "Seek My face!" Oh what an unearthly enticement! Do we heed such a challenge, such a commission, such an invitation? Or do we simply read an ancient book, viewing the naked relationship from afar, never daring to move with passionate longing toward this same God? God is not satisfied with passivity and religiosity. He desires more genuine and authentic joining and mingling of personalities.

Indulge a personal paraphrase of verse 4: "One thing, only one thing do I really desire. That one thing I will seek after passionately. To dwell, to live, to set up house in God's house for the rest of my life. To gaze upon His beauty, to be captivated, mesmerized by His presence. And in that privileged place, to inquire of the Lord." If we could have the same perspective as David, how different, more exciting, and more full of faith our inquiry with the Lord would be. Perhaps the mystery of Ephesians 3:20 would be more abundantly realized—"Now to him who is able to do immeasurably more than all we ask or imagine, according to his power that is at work in us" (NIV)—and our limited asking would probe further into the realm of dreaming, imagining, and thinking.

May my confidence in God's intervention approach that of David as I engage Him who is fully present in each and every circumstance, battle, and challenge of my life.

Practice

Writing Prompts

» Remember to begin with the question, "Lord, what would it sound like if You spoke this psalm to me personally?"

» In the face of enemies, fear is quelled because God is your Stronghold to run to, your Warrior and Protector who substitutes you out of the fray. Be sure to write this from the first-person perspective of God. Here is a suggested beginning: "Because you know Me, because you increasingly know Me better and better, together with David you too can say . . ."

» Develop verse 4 to capture the purification of this "one desire," this "one thing" that David sought after.

» Enjoy rewriting the rest of this psalm in the first person!

Devotional Thoughts

» Verses 1-3 speak strongly against fear. Yet many of us live with significant fear that drives us away from the beauty of verse 4: "One thing have I asked of the Lord . . . that I may dwell in the house of the Lord . . . to behold and gaze upon the beauty . . . of the Lord and to meditate, . . . in His temple" (AMP). Would you take a moment to listen to the Lord, seeking how He would name and call out those fears that plague you? Write your fears down.

» Now focus on verse 4. Expand verse 4 with the help of other translations and Bible-study helps. See the fullness and the power of David's confident relationship with God.

» Tell God that this is what you want. You don't know how to get there. Your fears still haunt you, but you long for this to be your "one desire." Pray this for days and weeks. Observe what happens in your confidence of this powerful relationship with God growing and expanding.

» Can you see yourself together with God, looking across at your fears? Can you see your debilitating fears as profoundly small in light of the great and mighty God you are partnered with? Write some in your journal about this fresh perspective.

CHAPTER 7

PSALM 34
Taste and See

Psalm 34 (NET)

I will praise the Lord at all times;
my mouth will continually praise him.
I will boast in the Lord;
let the oppressed hear and rejoice!
Magnify the Lord with me!
Let's praise his name together!
I sought the Lord's help and he answered me;
he delivered me from all my fears.
Those who look to him for help are happy;
their faces are not ashamed.
This oppressed man cried out and the Lord heard;
he saved him from all his troubles.
The Lord's angel camps around
the Lord's loyal followers and delivers them.
Taste and see that the Lord is good!
How blessed is the one who takes shelter in him!

Remain loyal to the LORD, you chosen people of his,
for his loyal followers lack nothing!
Even young lions sometimes lack food and
    are hungry,
but those who seek the LORD lack no good thing.
Come children! Listen to me!
I will teach you what it means to fear the LORD.
Do you want to really live?
Would you love to live a long, happy life?
Then make sure you don't speak evil words
or use deceptive speech!
Turn away from evil and do what is right!
Strive for peace and promote it!
The LORD pays attention to the godly
and hears their cry for help.
But the LORD opposes evildoers
and wipes out all memory of them from
    the earth.
The godly cry out and the LORD hears;
he saves them from all their troubles.
The LORD is near the brokenhearted;
he delivers those who are discouraged.
The godly face many dangers,
but the LORD saves them from each one of them.
He protects all his bones;
not one of them is broken.
Evil people self-destruct;
those who hate the godly are punished.
The LORD rescues his servants;
all who take shelter in him escape punishment.

Most are familiar with the phrase "taste and see that the Lord is good." Sandwiched between exaltation and crying out to the Lord for deliverance, this mantra invites us to experience God. It's fascinating that "taste" is the sense invoked for engaging more deeply with God. It's one thing for someone to describe for you how good the Lord is. We sing about His goodness. We read about His goodness. But just as when someone describes a delicious morsel to you, you cannot know something personally until you put the bite into your mouth and chew! A bite should be savored, not swallowed quickly. The meal should be a drawn-out, enjoyable experience. Much as Jeremiah expresses in Jeremiah 15:16, "Your words were found and I ate them, and Your words became for me a joy and the delight of my heart; for I have been called by Your name, O LORD God of hosts." We taste the Lord in His words. We taste the Lord in our joy. We taste the Lord in pain. We taste the Lord in others. God invites us to taste and see that He is good.

Psalm 34 in the First Person

I know that when you genuinely focus on Me, when you soak in My presence, kneeling before Me is a natural response. In such moments I extend My hand to your head and bestow a blessing. Love surges through My veins when you truly take time to adjust yourself to being with Me.

My heart swells when you declare your pride in Me. I watch satisfied as those downcast, afflicted, poor ones hear your boast and rejoice with you. They too are lifted up on the wings of your dedication to Me.

Still others gather around your uniting call. A groundswell of rejoicing expands as eager voices join the celebration around Me. Raucous exaltation rises to bless My soul as My people enjoy lifting high My names.

I answered you when you sought Me. It's just like I promised Jeremiah: "When you seek Me with your whole heart, I will let you find Me." Look to Me and your fears will shrink in comparison. I am here to deliver you!

When you look to Me, rays of My glory burst forth from your face. Just like Moses, you reflect My glory when you remain in My presence. With My glory on your face, there is no room for embarrassment or humiliation. Here there is no shame.

I hear when the poor and afflicted cry to me. I save them out of all anguish and distress.

My angel has pitched his tent close by those who fear Me. He is on guard and vigilant to rescue them.

Get your taste buds ready for a shockingly delicious treat! Taste Me! Get a good mouthful. Swirl the wine to expose all your taste buds. Enjoy. Savor the flavor. I am good. Taste and see for yourself! Blessed is the one who trusts deeply in Me, having tasted and now extending faith because they genuinely know Me more intimately.

Perhaps you fear many things. Exchange those fears for one pure and holy fear of Me. Experience the push-pull of My character inviting you with my mercy and forgiveness, yet repelling you with My glory. Stand in awe of the kaleidoscope of My incomprehensible presence. Experience wanting nothing else because you find that I fully satisfy your soul. Observe young lions just learning to hunt for themselves, often suffering grumbling bellies because their prey is more skilled in escaping than they are cunning in hunting. Not so with you. Seek Me, and you will be in want of no good thing. Come near, children. Listen attentively. Be a learner. Fearing Me is an excellent, life-changing lesson.

Do you want to really live? I have come that you might have amazing, abundant, and full life! But really experiencing My good life is in stark contrast to the world. Guard your tongue from the wickedness, deceit, and full-on evil of this world. Don't engage. Don't even give evil the time of day.

Avoid evil like the plague. Run from it! Do good! Run into the camp of peace! Pursue peace and wholeness. Your integrity depends on it.

I'm searching for the righteous ones. My ears are attuned to their cry. My help is poised and ready to rescue them from all trouble. But My face is opposed to evildoers. The memory of them will be like chaff blowing in the wind. Easily forgotten. In contrast, I hear and respond with deliverance to the cry of My righteous ones. I can hear their cry above all distractions and noise. Is your heart broken? Is your spirit crushed? Run to Me. I'm not far. I'm here to save.

Evil misery seems to plague you righteous ones. But I rescue you from every affliction. Even the details of your bones I preserve. No breakage because I am on watch. However, evil will turn on the wicked and attack them like a wild animal. They thought they would tame the beast. But evil is not tamable. It is an ancient, cruel master. The wicked hate the righteous. Their hatred is their sentence of death.

I am constantly on vigil to rescue My kids. Hide in Me and your worries are over. Condemnation will never come near your door. Relax and rest in Me.

Reflections

Writing Psalm 34 was wonderful because it was like visiting with an old friend. Yet it was written "in the cracks" as I went through a normal week, fitting in short periods of reflection. Not every psalm will be a mountaintop experience, but connecting with God in quiet moments of reflection will always be rich and rewarding. Allow God to speak to you in every context, even in the mundane and often busy schedule.

I was gripped by God's perspective on the first few verses. Usually I think in terms of the effect focusing on God has in my life. But here, God expresses His pleasure as the psalmist focuses on Him in light of very difficult circumstances, circumstances that would ordinarily scream for our attention. Then to see so many people around the psalmist who are drawn into a deeper experience with God because the psalmist has chosen to focus on the Lord is an added blessing.

I've loved "taste and see that the Lord is good" for many years. God creatively invites us to go beyond our intellectual connection with Him and plunges us into one of the five senses. To taste implies my risky commitment to move toward God and sample a morsel. God fully intends for me to be free to taste for myself, just as David and other psalmists experienced God in unique, outside-the-box ways. Will I just sit back and observe God from a distance, or will I sit down at the table and indulge in the banquet He spreads in front of me? The choice is mine. The invitation has been given.

And how do you exchange the fears of the world that so often plague us for one pure and holy fear of God? That's the million-dollar question. Fear is a subject that runs throughout Scripture—and God's continual exhortation is, "Do not fear!" Yet from a human perspective, we have many very good reasons to be afraid. We could find ourselves shouting back to God, "That's easy for You to say!" But perhaps with the focus on God that we see in Psalm 34, we can look at fear of things in the world from a different perspective. I'm reminded of a phrase out of Psalm 23: "Even when I must walk through the darkest valley, I fear no danger, for you are with me; your rod and your staff reassure me" (NET). We may always face scary times. But the truth is, God never leaves us. What a reassuring awareness. If I live a life focused on God, the beautiful new mind-set of God Himself helps me overcome my paralysis due to fear.

Practice

Writing Prompts

» Try to visualize the context of the first few verses from God's perspective: "Praise the Lord . . . boast in the Lord . . . magnify the Lord . . ." Attempt to get into God's heart as so much worship is surrounding Him. What would it sound like if He spoke these verses Himself? Perhaps something like, "A smile lights up My face as I receive your praise. My foot taps to the beat of your worship. I extend My Holy Spirit to set you free to worship Me with no inhibitions. I love your genuine worship."

» Keeping in mind the phrase "taste and see . . ." imagine a banquet feast that the Lord has invited you to. See Him as the Host. You are an honored guest at His table. How would He describe the meal?

» After the psalmist says, "Do you want to really live?" the subject of avoiding evil is introduced. Can you see God as a loving, caring Father who deeply desires for His children to experience the fullness of life? What would His voice sound like in covering these important instructions about avoiding evil?

» Enjoy rewriting the rest of this psalm in the first person!

Devotional Thoughts

» Reflecting on verses 1-3, express your deep desire to worship the Lord from the depths of your being: spirit, soul, mind, and strength. Hear the Lord calling you into His presence, enabling worship to be a natural response to Him.

» Consider the current difficulty or trouble you are in. Pore over verses 4-7. Allow God to weave your circumstances into this exercise of tasting Him more deeply.

» Explore the sense of "tasting" the Lord (verse 8). How does your imagination connect with this invitation from the Lord? Consider exploring other senses, like seeing and smelling the Lord!

» Renew your commitment to avoid evil and those promoting evil.

» Meditate on verses 9-14. What if you grew to fear less and less due to your relationship with God? What if you had just one pure and holy fear of God Himself growing within you in strength and power? The fear of God is not just raw terror. And the word for fear throughout the Bible does not mean "be afraid"! Let me be quick to say, this is a deep and complex subject that cannot be adequately addressed in this context. Yet for the sake of more fully experiencing God, you may want to look at Isaiah 6:1-8. Isaiah found himself in the midst of a magnificent vision of God's throne room. Angels were flying around shouting, "Holy, holy, holy is the Lord of hosts, the whole earth is full of His glory!" The building was shaking and filling with smoke. Then Isaiah cried out, "I'm a dead man! I have filthy lips, and the people around me have filthy lips. And I've seen the King, the Lord of hosts. And no one sees the King and lives to tell about it!" (author's paraphrase). Then an angel took a burning coal from the fire in front of God (how hot is that fire?) and flew straight toward Isaiah. The angel touched Isaiah's lips and cleansed his sin. Isaiah's terrifying engagement with God changed drastically. What was earlier a sure-death situation became calm after the storm of cleansing and forgiveness. Then God spoke: "Whom shall I send, and who will go for Us?" Isaiah found himself invited into partnership with God to deliver His message to the people. Can you see how God converts a genuine fearful experience with Him into a powerful ministry partnership? This is often the place I go to sort through at least some of what God means to "fear Him."

» Take some time to paraphrase Isaiah 6:1-8 in your journal. Allow God to take your pen and add other cross-references from Scripture to paint a fuller picture. Be sure to add the reality of Jesus and His new covenant in contrast to the Old Testament context of Isaiah's experience.

» As you read verses 15-18, consider how you might hear the Lord express His attentiveness to your life and circumstances.

CHAPTER 8

PSALM 42

What Do You Do with Despair?

Psalm 42 (NIV)

For the director of music. A maskil of the Sons of Korah.

As the deer pants for streams of water,
    so my soul pants for you, my God.
My soul thirsts for God, for the living God.
    When can I go and meet with God?
My tears have been my food
    day and night,
while people say to me all day long,
    "Where is your God?"
These things I remember
    as I pour out my soul:
how I used to go to the house of God
    under the protection of the Mighty One
with shouts of joy and praise
    among the festive throng.

Why, my soul, are you downcast?
    Why so disturbed within me?
Put your hope in God,
    for I will yet praise him,
    my Savior and my God.

My soul is downcast within me;
    therefore I will remember you
from the land of the Jordan,
    the heights of Hermon—from Mount Mizar.
Deep calls to deep
    in the roar of your waterfalls;
all your waves and breakers
    have swept over me.

By day the LORD directs his love,
    at night his song is with me —
    a prayer to the God of my life.

I say to God my Rock,
    "Why have you forgotten me?
Why must I go about mourning,
    oppressed by the enemy?"
My bones suffer mortal agony
    as my foes taunt me,
saying to me all day long,
    "Where is your God?"

Why, my soul, are you downcast?
    Why so disturbed within me?

Put your hope in God,
> for I will yet praise him,
> my Savior and my God.

Dire circumstances have caused the psalmist to lose perspective on God. How can he possibly find God again in the midst of such disillusionment? Yet God has taught this God-seeker to remember his milestones. What are the markers that point him to God?

Do not allow your circumstances to determine for you who God is and where God is. Let God be who He says He is, and adjust your belief to that anchor! You see, we have an anchor that actually goes behind the veil, where God is (Hebrews 6:19)! Your little boat may be bobbing on the ocean of life's turmoil, but be careful that you don't cut the rope to your anchor by allowing your circumstances to dictate to you who God is.

We feel comforted by the old song taken from this psalm: "As the deer panteth for the water, so my soul longeth after Thee . . ." Yet the context of this psalm is life-threatening chaos! This deer is running for its life. In an emotional sense, we may experience such feelings of exhaustion, fear, and hopelessness. It's fascinating that the psalmist stops in the midst of his tears and anguish to talk to his soul. In this psalm, the psalmist makes a significant transformation from the depths of misery to the solid ground of faith and trust in God. May God instruct us to make such a beautiful and powerful adjustment from earth to heaven when life is falling apart.

Psalm 42 in the First Person

The hunted deer, pursued by dogs, famished and terrified, longs to stop for a cool drink. I know that's similar to the way you long for Me, the living God, the Source of rest for your exhausted being. You long to slow down, look into My face, gain perspective, taste refreshing water. But you dare not stop. You know your enemies would easily overtake you.

You've been wondering if you will ever find your way back to Me. Perspective is lost, yet I'm right here. I haven't gone anywhere, regardless of your sense of My presence. Come. Come to Me. You're dying of inner thirst that can only be satisfied in Me. Drink deeply of Me. Fill your parched soul at the fountain of My living water!

Eyes sore, tears flowing, day and night, night and day—salty weeping seasons your hunger. The Enemy taunts you: "Where is this God of yours now, God-seeker?" You look but can't find Me. The jeers haunt your sensitive ears.

Pouring out your soul, you mysteriously remember favorite events, markers when you experienced Me richly. Singing, shouting expressions of joy and gratitude, you led worshipers into My presence! Your memories flood in, giving you hope and courage.

You look deep inside, saying to your soul, "Why are you in despair? Why are you causing such disturbance and turmoil within me? Put your hope in God! I will praise Him once again! Surely His presence is here to help me!" I agree with your soul-correction. Now you are looking beyond the human dilemma. Now you are gaining hope!

Then you turn to talk to Me, frustrated with your soul. Deep wisdom is working, penetrating your heart. You remember significant road signs from your journey with Me, signposts where I revealed Myself to you. The land of Jordan, the peaks of Hermon, Mount Mizar. Hope grows as you remember Me in the context of your chaos and despair.

Deep harmonizes with deep, brooks resonate with streams, My message of love and care begins to overwhelm you. Waves crash, waterfalls thunder, speaking of My presence and faithfulness. By day, My lovingkindness soothes you by night, My songs wash over you.

Anguish cries out to Me. You feel like I've forgotten you. But I'm very aware of your enemy's oppression and aggression. Taunts and mocking reach My ears day and night. I too hear them say, "Where is your God now, believer?" But what do you believe? Do you remember the truth? The truth can set you free.

You look deep inside, saying to your soul, "Why are you in despair? Why are you causing such disturbance and turmoil within me? Put your hope in God! I will praise Him once again! Surely His presence is here to help me!" Yes, I agree with your soul-correction. You are learning to look beyond the human dilemma. Your circumstances do not determine who I am.

Reflections

The picture is vivid. The stag, chased by dogs and hunters, panting for cool water but not daring to stop for a drink. Life depends on continuing to run!

Do you ever feel like you have to keep running? Sometimes it seems like the world has turned against us. Mocking, ridicule, and shame attack at every turn. We can't see God in our current surroundings. But isn't God who He says He is, regardless of our situation? We want to believe, but immediate stress is in our face, preventing us from seeing God. The psalmist seems to be able to make this difficult emotional shift. How can we learn from him?

The psalmist had life markers, milestones, piles of rocks like those God instructed the Israelites to erect throughout the Old Testament. The psalmist looked back at his markers when life fell apart and despair set in. He reminded himself. He remembered.

How can the psalmist shift so quickly from despair to hope? I tend to get a shovel out and dig a deeper hole for myself when despair sets in. Could we choose the psalmist's course? What are our markers to look back on? What are those defining moments in our histories when God revealed Himself to us profoundly? What God said to us last still stands until He speaks again!

God really is concerned for our heart and soul. I mentioned earlier that the entire human drama is contained in the Psalms. We can go to the Psalms to learn how to properly engage with God regardless of our emotional state. We don't have to perform or pretend we are doing well.

In this psalm, God appears to be communicating His love for us, His faithfulness, in our soul, in water, in mountains. Are you listening? Or is your despair drowning out the message of hope? God spoke to Elijah in a "still small voice." Can you listen carefully and hear His voice today?

Self-talk can often take on a very nasty, negative tenor. Typically we slip back into believing lies that are ingrained in our thought patterns. But here, self-talk resets the psalmist to a strongly positive, truthful, hopeful perspective that bombards his despair. Positive, biblical self-talk, soul-talk can be practiced to overcome the depths of anguish and confusion. Do you need to give your soul a good talking-to?

Practice

Writing Prompts

» Consider this beginning: "Deer long for cool brooks to quench their parched throats, especially when they are hunted. What about your soul? Do you long for Me in a similar way?"

» Reflect on verse 3. Have you ever been ridiculed for believing in God? Can you relive that experience and enter into the psalmist's emotions as you listen to God speak to you personally from the taunting mockery? Here are several suggestions to get you started: "You cry yourself to sleep at night, listening to the jeers of your friends. At least you thought they were your friends." Or, "Even your parents mocked you today for believing in Me!" Or, "Your tears splash in My presence as I stand by your side in the midst of scornful mocking."

» When the psalmist shifts to talk to his soul—"Why, my soul, are you downcast? Why so disturbed within me?"—imagine God overhearing this unusual soul talking-to. But God is pleased. How might this sound from God's perspective? Consider: "I'm so pleased with your soul talk. Instead of listening to the lies of that evil one, you wrestle with . . ."

» Then the psalmist turns from talking to his soul to talking to God about his soul: "My soul is downcast within me, therefore I remember You . . ." and later, "I say to God my Rock . . ." How might God further engage after hearing this God-seeker adjust his soul? Perhaps, "Now you are talking to the very Source of Life! Remember what I said in Psalm 23—'I restore your soul'? Well, come here; let me do the spiritual surgery needed to restore your despairing soul."

» Enjoy rewriting the rest of this psalm in the first person!

Devotional Thoughts

» Have you ever talked to your soul? Sounds a little crazy! Perhaps you are in a good frame of mind and emotions currently. From this positive posture, how would you construct a good talking-to that would serve to adjust your despairing soul back to God at a later time? Perhaps something like, "O my soul, listen to me! My God is still on His throne! I can't see Him in my current circumstances, but that doesn't mean He has abandoned me!" How would you continue this soul speech?

» Think back over your life. Identify your milestones, your markers, your "piles of rocks" that are there to remind you of significant events with God in your journey. Summarize these signposts for future reference to help you remember God when your current circumstances cause you to despair. Insert three of your highlights with God into verse 6, filling in the blanks: "I hear your soul cry out to Me in despair. I wait for you to remember those wonderful, memorable events to regain your footing. Do you remember _____, _____, and _____? You said you would never forget those life-changing encounters with Me."

CHAPTER 9

PSALM 46
Be Still and Know God

Psalm 46 (NLT)

God is our refuge and strength,
   always ready to help in times of trouble.
So we will not fear when earthquakes come
   and the mountains crumble into the sea.
Let the oceans roar and foam.
      Let the mountains tremble as the waters surge!
A river brings joy to the city of our God,
   the sacred home of the Most High.
God dwells in that city; it cannot be destroyed.
      From the very break of day, God will protect it.
The nations are in chaos,
   and their kingdoms crumble!
God's voice thunders,
   and the earth melts!
The LORD of Heaven's Armies is here among us;
   the God of Israel is our fortress.

Come, see the glorious works of the LORD:
　See how he brings destruction upon the world.
He causes wars to end throughout the earth.
　He breaks the bow and snaps the spear;
　he burns the shields with fire.
"Be still, and know that I am God!
　I will be honored by every nation.
　I will be honored throughout the world."
The LORD of Heaven's Armies is here among us;
　the God of Israel is our fortress.

The Lord of hosts is with us; the God of Jacob is our stronghold. God's people are safe within the walls of His city, and they exude security and confidence. The conquering King establishes His city as the ultimate safe haven. When nations rise up against Him, He speaks and the earth does His bidding. No enemy stands a chance against such power and authority.

Psalm 46 in the First Person

This is My city. You are My people. I am the safe place you can run to during troubling times. I am your strength, and I make you strong. I vigilantly stand guard, always ready to help when you need Me.

Due to this sure belief, your fear is dispelled. Even though the earth itself should shift and shake, no fear. Even though mountains crumble and fall into the seas, no fear. Even though the waters roar and churn, no fear. Even though mountains tremble at the swelling pride of mighty waters, no fear.

In My city, there is a river whose streams bring joy and gladness to all, flourishing growth. Even to those who dip their feet for coolness, joy and gladness. Even for those who listen to the laughing waters, joy and gladness. Even for those who ride its currents, joy and gladness. This is My dwelling place, the home of God Most High. Welcome home.

I walk through the midst of My city. She is secure, unshakable. I am right there to help as morning dawns, as dusk descends.

Surrounding nations rise up, ranting and raging. Then they stumble. I speak and earth melts, quickly obeying My command; earthquake, tsunami, volcano.

I am here, the Lord of mighty hosts, the Stronghold of My people from beginning until now.

Come near, observe My works. I establish horrors, desolations, destruction against My enemies.

I make wars to cease by crushing those who would make war. I break their bows. I chop their spears. I burn the war wagons so battle is not possible!

Stop! Do nothing. Be quiet. Let all striving cease. Now, know Me, experience Me. Receive from Me what you cannot do for yourself in truly knowing Me. In these surrounding nations, I will be exalted. Yes, I will be exalted in all the earth! But you My child, be still and know Me.

I am here, the Lord of mighty hosts, the Stronghold of My people from beginning until now.

Reflections

I love the phrase "a very present help in trouble." Several translations use these words for verse 1. God is not just present—He is *very* present. Once again, strong confidence over enemies comes from strong faith in God's presence and promise.

The river of God brings joy to the city of God. Rivers bring transportation, trade, life, food, recreation, and other wonderful benefits. The picture of the river attending the city of God is favored and pleasant. Cities with multiple rivers merging have a magnetic draw to my soul. Waterways are so often spoken of as examples of God's blessing.

God's city is planted right in the middle of the chaos of surrounding nations. God's city and God's people are on display for the world to see. And God is all about stopping war. Yet war is often necessary to stop tyranny. Ultimately God will wipe out all warmongers and bring peace, true peace among men. And in the midst of war and rumors of war, God says, "Be still, and know Me."

"Be still and know that I am God" has captured my attention for decades. How can we know God, even experience God better, if our only responsibility is to do nothing? The very strong implication is that God must be going to do something. God carries the primary responsibility for my knowing Him. What a restful and encouraging thought.

Practice

Writing Prompts

» Hear God speaking of Himself in the midst of earthquakes and hurricanes. I would suggest, "The chaos and turmoil of natural disasters are only an opportunity for Me to display . . ."

» Now God shifts emphasis to His city. Listen as He describes the beauty, the location, the magnificence of the city of God: "Welcome to My city. Let Me take you on a tour of the greatest city ever imagined! Observe . . ."

» Then God shifts to the rebelling nations outlying His city. Hear Him speak of the anarchy and how He deals with it: "Nations rise, kingdoms fall. Some think they will last much longer, perhaps forever; then My voice thunders . . ."

» Various translations render the word for "be still" as *stop, let go, relax, cease striving*. Use these words (and even more) to capture God's heart for His people. His passion is for them to know Him, to deeply, relationally know Him. But He begins with, "Be still, stop, enough, relax, and . . ."

» Enjoy rewriting the rest of this psalm in the first person!

Devotional Thoughts

» Does your relationship with God (verse 1) allow you to share the psalmist's convictions (verse 2)? Does genuinely knowing God help you properly rein in dominating fear?

» How many different ways can you say, "Do nothing"? Do you really believe that if you do nothing, that if you are still, relaxed, stopped, God will take initiative for you to know Him more deeply? Explore this mystery further.

CHAPTER 10

PSALM 51
The Penitent Sinner Seeks Forgiveness

Psalm 51 (NASB)

Be gracious to me, O God, according to Your
    lovingkindness;
According to the greatness of Your compassion
    blot out my transgressions.
Wash me thoroughly from my iniquity
And cleanse me from my sin.
For I know my transgressions,
And my sin is ever before me.
Against You, You only, I have sinned
And done what is evil in Your sight,
So that You are justified when You speak
And blameless when You judge.
Behold, I was brought forth in iniquity,
And in sin my mother conceived me.
Behold, You desire truth in the innermost being,
And in the hidden part You will make me know wisdom.

Purify me with hyssop, and I shall be clean;
Wash me, and I shall be whiter than snow.
Make me to hear joy and gladness,
Let the bones which You have broken rejoice.
Hide Your face from my sins
And blot out all my iniquities.
Create in me a clean heart, O God,
And renew a steadfast spirit within me.
Do not cast me away from Your presence
And do not take Your Holy Spirit from me.
Restore to me the joy of Your salvation
And sustain me with a willing spirit.
Then I will teach transgressors Your ways,
And sinners will be converted to You.
Deliver me from bloodguiltiness, O God,
        the God of my salvation;
Then my tongue will joyfully sing of Your righteousness.
O Lord, open my lips,
That my mouth may declare Your praise.
For You do not delight in sacrifice, otherwise
        I would give it;
You are not pleased with burnt offering.
The sacrifices of God are a broken spirit;
A broken and a contrite heart, O God,
        You will not despise.
By Your favor do good to Zion;
Build the walls of Jerusalem.
Then You will delight in righteous sacrifices,
In burnt offering and whole burnt offering;
Then young bulls will be offered on Your altar.

David stood on his rooftop late at night, watching a beautiful woman bathing. She was another man's wife. David was supposed to be at war with the army. This woman's husband was one of David's mighty warriors—not just an ordinary guy, but one deeply devoted to David. David took the woman for his own pleasure. She became pregnant. Then David tried to cover it up by having her husband come back from war to sleep with her. But Uriah was an honorable man and wouldn't enjoy intimacy with his wife if his comrades were not afforded such pleasure. So David plotted to have Uriah killed.

Nathan, God's prophet, told David a story about a ruthless rich man who stole everything from a less fortunate man. Ultimately, David condemned the man portrayed in the prophecy of Nathan for his cruel and selfish actions. Then Nathan said, "You are the man!" Thus began David's heartfelt repentance for his sin against God. May we all find heartbreak and passion as we come to grips with our sin, seeing it as God sees it.

Psalm 51 in the First Person

My heart is broken over your sin against Me. Yet the wealth of My mercy rises up for you. My strong and perfect love reaches out to you. Compassion flows from My heart to wash you, cleanse you, restore you, to completely cover your sin. I will erase all memory of your rebellious acts. Even the guilt of your sin is cleansed and forgiven so that you might be purified and made whole again. I have made you painfully aware of the magnitude of your sin against Me, and you have responded with heartfelt, genuine repentance. You know Me. You know that I am here with all the resources of heaven to restore you and to rebuild our relationship. You are not flippant about the impact of your sin on our relationship. I am grieved over your sin, yet pleased with your broken heart. Yes, you have sinned grievously against your fellow man. However, you are deeply aware that ultimately your sin is against Me—against Me alone! You have rebelled and dishonored Me, turned your back on Me, and done what is evil in My sight. I am completely justified in sentencing you, faultless in judging you. I alone am God. I alone have the power to forgive. No one questions My judgment. Neither do they dare stand up in My court. The full extent of your sinful choices is completely on display before Me. I am appalled. I am disgusted. And you are too.

Observe: you were born a sinner. Observe: I delight in faithfulness and integrity ruling in your hidden heart, those places where sin and righteousness struggle for domination. I want you to possess moral insight and ethical craftsmanship. I am present to help you overcome those passionate surges that overtake your character. You are not alone in this fight.

Forgiveness is what you seek. And you have come to the only Source of forgiveness. You long for spiritual cleansing, hyssop sprinkling water. You long for soul cleansing, washed whiter than snow. You have come to the Cleanser, to the Forgiver, to the Healer. When you wallow in your sin, your ears are tuned only to self-deprecation and condemning dirge. You miss worshiping Me. But I will speak magnified joy and gladness to your heart once again. Your sin is to you like crushed bones. But I will free those crushed bones to rejoice again. You are embarrassed to be in My presence clothed in sin. You wish you could hide! But I will exchange those rags for a pure white robe. Once again My face will be reflected in your face.

You've come to the Creator for the shaping and molding of a fresh and pure heart. Not only will I do as you have pleaded, but I will renew and repair an even stronger and resolute spirit within you! I will also restore to you the first joy of My salvation! I will deliver you from the guilt of bloodshed. I am the God of your salvation. I will make you the kind of person who wants to obey. Your heart cry is for Me to not cast you away from My presence, that I would not remove My Holy Spirit from you. For David, this *was a terrifying possibility. He had witnessed My abandonment of Saul! But you are secure beyond anything David knew or dreamed of. He only tasted the covenant that was to come. But you have feasted on My new covenant. Never will I leave you! Never will I forsake you! So do not spurn My merciful forgiveness.*

Once I have completed this life-altering work in you, humbly help others with the same restoration I have given you. Teach them My ways. Return them to Me.

I am blessed as you transform due to My deliverance. I love it as your heart begins to joyfully sing again. I watch you shed those filthy clothes and exchange them for My righteous robe. Here, let Me anoint your lips to express fully the praise welling up in your heart. You know that I do not take delight in some rote, ancient, and external form of sacrifice. I don't want penance. I'm after true heart change. I want your spirit to be broken over your sin. When you pour out a broken and crushed heart due to your sin, I will not loathe or reject it. That's when true spiritual transformation begins to take root!

(Note: I chose not to include verses 18-19.)

Reflections

I've often wrestled with the phrase "Against You, You only, have I sinned and done what is evil in Your sight." After all, David clearly sinned against Bathsheba and Uriah. He even conspired to have Uriah killed. He drew Joab into his evil and unrepentant plot. Other innocent soldiers were likely killed as though they were expendable. Even then David had no remorse until he was caught red-handed by Nathan!

But his mantra, "Against You, You only have I sinned," was

piercingly unveiled as I began to understand it in the course of my own ungodly patterns. The broken view I had of myself and the world caused me to interpret life quite differently from how those concerned with my inaccurate perspective discerned life. Friends and loved ones tried to help me see my actions as they saw them. I disagreed, thinking that I understood not only their point of view but my own flawed interpretation. Looking back, I see the arrogance and fallacy of not listening to those who cared for me. Just a small dose of humility would have caused me to submit my point of view to theirs. This pride continued for years! Then God mercifully intervened and spoke profoundly and undeniably to me through two authors and a loving, gifted counselor. Through them God said, "You have truly sinned against Me in the way your friends have described." I was dumbfounded! How could I have been so blind? But now God had my attention. He is faithful to pursue me even when I am obstinate and hardheaded.

Gripped with the magnitude of my sin, I journaled for weeks before actually "doing business with God." The authors and my friend had given me a new language to capture the truth of this revelation. Once I was ready to genuinely go to God with my process of repentance, words formed in my heart just before I put pen to paper. I intended to write, "Lord, I've sinned against You and against my loved one." But as the ink flowed to form, "Lord, I've sinned against You . . ." God interrupted my course. He said, "Stop right there!" I literally put the pen down! God continued, "You have sinned against Me and Me alone!" Immediately Psalm 51 came front and center as though projected on a screen. For days I pored over David's contrition, making it my own, expressing my humility, shame, and regret over my sin against God. Yes, I had sinned against my loved ones as well. And perhaps as before, I had said a sincere but quick "I'm sorry" to God while focusing extensively and quickly on the person I had hurt so deeply. I had a common pattern of prematurely transitioning from acknowledging my sin against God to more thoroughly dealing with my sin against a very present person. After all, I needed to make things right with this person and restore our relationship due to my insensitivity. God was . . . well, He was God. I said I was sorry. I meant it too. God didn't want me groveling in penance in order to be forgiven. But this was different. I had never dwelt on my sin against God long enough to allow the effect on our relationship to sink in. Now, for the first time God had taken initiative and stopped me to realize what David meant when he said, "Against You, You only have I sinned."

My repentance was deeper and more sincere than ever before. So genuine and transformational was my change that soon, others began to experience me in an entirely different way. The most profound evidence was that I began to experience myself as freed from the bondage of my past patterns. I had changed in ways that I never thought possible. But my changes were simply the byproduct of true repentance. And it all began with seeing my sin as God sees it. True repentance seems to have beautiful and powerful ongoing benefits.

Practice

Writing Prompts

» Right away David throws himself on God's safe character. Consider this beginning from God's point of view: "Your cry for mercy opens My door to you in the midst of your mess. You are right and wise to call on My lovingkindness, on My unfailing love. You know how I love you. And My compassion is essential for you in these circumstances of your profound failure."

» Reread verse 4: "Against You, and You only have I sinned . . ." Can you hear God say, "Your sin, your plotting and conniving sin, O favored one, is a smear on our relationship. I am deeply wounded that you would go to such lengths to satisfy your sexual urges. Have I not blessed you with . . ."

» Verse 10 begins, "Create in me a clean heart . . ." From God's perspective, this might sound like, "I must perform spiritual surgery on your heart. Sign the waiver, and I will do an open-heart procedure that will conform you even more into My image. And your spirit, here let Me . . ."

» Enjoy rewriting the rest of this psalm in the first person!

Devotional Thoughts

» This is perhaps the most vulnerable I have ever been in expressing a psalm in the first person. Be very careful of launching a witch hunt in your own heart and soul over past sins. That is the work of the Holy Spirit. He alone convicts of sin, righteousness, and judgment (John 16:7-8). Listen to Him and respond to all that He reveals. Trust Him and put one foot in front of the other.

» Meditate on David's famous statement: "Against You, You only have I sinned." Read 2 Samuel 11:1–12:14. Soak in this story for a period of time. Don't be in a hurry to write. Allow the Lord to speak to you. How does Psalm 51 capture this relational truth between God and His chosen one?

» Reread Psalm 51:6-9, and deeply consider the heart of God and His desires for you. Listen well in multiple translations.

» "Create in me a clean heart, O God, and renew a steadfast spirit within me." Once again, a well-known heart cry to the God who forgives. As we plead with God for restoration and healing from our sin, how might God express this human dilemma from His point of view?

» Verse 11 reveals the contrast between God's old and new covenant. Considering the profound, finished work of Jesus on the cross, what is our new position and standing with God?

» Verses 15-17 lead us into worship and praise. Spend some time worshiping God for His forgiveness. Give to God the sacrifice He accepts: your humble and broken heart and spirit.

CHAPTER 11

PSALM 62
Wait in Silence for God Only

Psalm 62 (ESV)

For God alone my soul waits in silence;
    from him comes my salvation.
He alone is my rock and my salvation,
    my fortress; I shall not be greatly shaken.
How long will all of you attack a man
    to batter him,
        like a leaning wall, a tottering fence?
They only plan to thrust him down from
        his high position.
    They take pleasure in falsehood.
They bless with their mouths,
    but inwardly they curse.
For God alone, O my soul, wait in silence,
    for my hope is from him.
He only is my rock and my salvation,
    my fortress; I shall not be shaken.

On God rests my salvation and my glory;
>   my mighty rock, my refuge is God.

Trust in him at all times, O people;
>   pour out your heart before him;
>   God is a refuge for us.

Those of low estate are but a breath;
>   those of high estate are a delusion;

in the balances they go up;
>   they are together lighter than a breath.

Put no trust in extortion;
>   set no vain hopes on robbery;
>   if riches increase, set not your heart on them.

Once God has spoken;
>   twice have I heard this:

that power belongs to God,
>   and that to you, O Lord, belongs steadfast love.

For you will render to a man
>   according to his work.

God—only. Seems like it's so easy, so natural to look for God and *something*. God and *anything* greatly diminishes God and His well-earned, proper place in our lives. What do we trust in? Our abilities? Our earning power? Our intellect? Do we really trust God only? This psalm is an invitation to examine those fleeting sources of security.

Psalm 62 in the First Person

For Me only, wait in silence, precious soul.
>   *Quiet your soul. Shalom. Anticipate Me.*
>   *Adjust yourself to the reality that you are in My presence.*

Listen. I'm here. I'm with you. You are not alone.

I speak to your soul. Do you hear Me? I woo your soul. I created your soul to be satisfied only with Me. I say to your soul, "Rest in Me. Wait in silence for Me only."

Only I deliver you.

Only I am your solid rock.

Only I am your Stronghold, your Strong Tower.

You will not be greatly shaken.

Your enemies gang up, hurling threats and insults at you. Trust Me for protection. You need My safety because your enemies are committed to your destruction! They will persist and pursue you to the bitter end. Some of your enemies are brash and in-your-face; others are subtle and difficult to detect. But I fight them all.

Your enemies don't realize they have one foot on a slippery slope into the pit. They will fall. Their destruction is inevitable.

And let Me be clear—they don't aim to hurt you. They aim to kill you! They take counsel among themselves regarding how to bring you down. They love lies. Their father is the father of lies. They may bless you with their mouth, but in their heart they curse you.

For Me only, be silent, precious soul!

Put your hope in Me only.

Only I am your rock, your safe place.

Only I deliver you.

Only I am your stronghold, your strong tower.

You will not be moved!

I deliver you.

I honor you.

You can be safe in Me, where no enemy can reach you.

Trust Me implicitly, always.

I'm eager for you to pour out your heart to Me.

I am your safe place, your hiding place.
Common people are but a breath.
Strong individuals are simply a mirage.
What or whom do you trust?
Is it man? Get ready to be disappointed.
Is it power? An illusion.
Is it oppression? What goes around comes around.
Is it money that you trust in? Like stocks it can crash to nothing.
They are all lightweight, frail, fleeting, like the wind.
They will all fail you. Do not set your heart on them.
I spoke once and made it very clear; twice you have heard Me:
All power belongs to Me. That's why I can say that I alone am the Rock.
And I am the Author of unfailing love. I love you perfectly.
I pay back people according to their deeds. I reward each person for
what they have done.

Reflections

I'm often intrigued when a word is inserted into a translation that is not actually in the original text. In verse 1, *wait* is not found in the original Hebrew. I respect translators for inserting necessary words to help us with the intention of sentence structure and meaning, but my curiosity is piqued. If *wait* is not in the text, what are the implications? How would the sentence be heard in the original Hebrew? Perhaps something like, "My soul is in silence before God only." I envision sitting expectantly at the foot of God's throne, patiently waiting, resting, anticipating God's initiative. And not only is the environment around me still, but I am calm and still on the inside, trusting, waiting, relaxed, expecting the voice of my closest friend, my confidante, and my advocate to touch my soul as only He can.

God provides safety, trust, and refuge for a weary soul. Life can get crazy. Everything around me can shake. My own life can shake significantly. He doesn't say I will not be shaken. He says I will not be *greatly* shaken! But God promises that my shaking will not result in my destruction. Praise the Lord! It's sort of like 1 Corinthians 10:13: "No temptation has overtaken you that is not common to man. God is faithful, and *He will not let you be tempted beyond your ability*, but with the temptation he will also provide the way of escape, that you may be able to endure it" (ESV). Yes, I will struggle. Yes, I will be tempted. But I wait in silence for God only. He is my Rock. He is my salvation. He is my fortress. I will not be greatly shaken!

There are powerful enemies bent on our destruction. They even take counsel among themselves to overthrow us! But God sees their scheming. He is never unaware. He has an entirely different end for them in mind, and in the face of intense opposition, God's presence as our Strong Tower of safety beckons us to security.

Examine all the possible avenues we might seek for security. Compare them all to God. It's ludicrous to trust anything or anyone but God alone!

Practice

Writing Prompts

» Imagine a completely soundproof environment with only you and God present. All distractions are eliminated. Then He says, "Shhhh. Quiet your soul. Still your anxious heart. Adjust yourself to My throne room. In My presence . . ." Finish the sentence.

» For each of the truth statements—"He alone is my rock. He alone is my salvation. He alone is my fortress . . ."—hear God embellish His identity with "I alone, no one else, am your solid and secure Rock. I alone, no one else, am your Savior, both ultimately and day to day. I alone, no one else, am . . ." Complete and expand God's announcement of His identity.

» Enjoy rewriting the rest of this psalm in the first person!

Devotional Thoughts

» Examine carefully, with God's help, your possible sources of safety and security. If you're not seeking safety and security from God alone, are you truly secure? Is safety only a mirage?

» Meditate on the "Only I . . ." phrases in my first-person rewrite. For instance, "Only I deliver you. Only I am your solid rock." Do you need to make some adjustments in your heart to exclusively lean on God for particular aspects of your need? Would it help to make your own "Only I . . ." list to remind yourself of your determined dependence on God alone? The inside flap of your Bible is a great place to record these reminders.

» Consider your opposition. Do you have a clear focus on God in the midst of insults, challenges, and danger? What can you do to see God more clearly? What can you do to see your enemy in proper perspective? But let's be careful of the question, "What can you do . . .?" when the real "doing" is done by God. Perhaps we should ask, "How can you trust God for . . . ?"

CHAPTER 12

PSALM 73

A Dangerous Comparison

Psalm 73 (NIV)

Surely God is good to Israel,
    to those who are pure in heart.
But as for me, my feet had almost slipped;
    I had nearly lost my foothold.
For I envied the arrogant
    when I saw the prosperity of the wicked.
They have no struggles;
    their bodies are healthy and strong.
They are free from the burdens common to man;
    they are not plagued by human ills.
Therefore pride is their necklace;
    they clothe themselves with violence.
From their callous hearts comes iniquity;
    the evil conceits of their minds know no limits.
They scoff, and speak with malice;
    in their arrogance they threaten oppression.

Their mouths lay claim to heaven,
    and their tongues take possession of the earth.
Therefore their people turn to them
    and drink up waters in abundance.
They say, "How can God know?
    Does the Most High have knowledge?"
This is what the wicked are like—
    always carefree, they increase in wealth.
Surely in vain have I kept my heart pure;
    in vain have I washed my hands in innocence.
All day long I have been plagued;
    I have been punished every morning.
If I had said, "I will speak thus,"
    I would have betrayed your children.
When I tried to understand all this,
    it was oppressive to me
till I entered the sanctuary of God;
    then I understood their final destiny.
Surely you place them on slippery ground;
    you cast them down to ruin.
How suddenly are they destroyed,
    completely swept away by terrors!
As a dream when one awakes,
    so when you arise, O Lord,
    you will despise them as fantasies.
When my heart was grieved
    and my spirit embittered,
I was senseless and ignorant;
    I was a brute beast before you.
Yet I am always with you;

you hold me by my right hand.
You guide me with your counsel,
    and afterward you will take me into glory.
Whom have I in heaven but you?
    And earth has nothing I desire besides you.
My flesh and my heart may fail,
    but God is the strength of my heart
    and my portion forever.
Those who are far from you will perish;
    you destroy all who are unfaithful to you.
But as for me, it is good to be near God.
    I have made the Sovereign LORD my refuge;
    I will tell of all your deeds.

Too often, we extract verses from their context—as often happens with this gut-wrenching psalm. Verses 25 and 26 are familiar: "Whom have I in heaven but You? And besides You, I desire nothing on earth. My flesh and my heart may fail, but God is the strength of my heart and my portion forever." We may fail to realize that these poetic phrases are found in the midst of the confused and precarious psalmist's observations regarding the ease and apparent well-being of the godless in the world. The psalmist had nearly slipped while dwelling on the lack of suffering he saw in the lives of the wealthy and arrogant. So often we may say, "If only I had more money . . . If only I had what my rich neighbor has . . . If only my life was as easy as theirs." Covetousness is a dangerous pill to swallow. Greed is the wicked motivator hidden deep within. Envy whispers dissatisfaction in our ear. We crave what someone else has. This writer came dangerously close to falling over the edge with his covetous gaze.

Psalm 73 in the First Person

It's a general statement, but true nonetheless: "I am good to My people. I am good to the pure in heart." But you may not feel like I'm very good to you in your personal circumstances, especially when you begin comparing your life to the lives of those embracing the world.

You wandered down a precarious trail, looking intently at the lifestyle and condition of the wicked. Your conclusions were skewed and flawed, yet you continued the comparison. You came dangerously close to stumbling. The ground under you morphed into a slippery slope. You turned green with envy as you considered the welfare and prosperity of the wicked. They boast arrogantly of how good their life is. You were beginning to believe them.

The wicked appear to have no pain, no restrictions to hold them back or cause them delay. Their bodies are strong and well fed. They live in the lap of luxury. They are immune to the trouble common to most people. Their life really is the good life! It appears that ordinary people can't even get close to them, touch them, or affect them at all. A bubble of privilege surrounds them and their kind.

Pride is the necklace adorning their collar in blatant display. Garments woven from the lives of those they step on as they climb the success ladder are their everyday apparel. No concern troubles them as they hurt and destroy others to achieve their goals.

Greed causes their eyes to bulge; lust and craving drools from their mouths as they anticipate new opportunities to climb even higher. Imaginations of their wicked hearts run riot with creative evil. Mocking all that is good, they spout sinful tirades on righteousness and everything that opposes them. From their elevated perch they pour oppression on everyone and everything below their high seats of power and control.

Speaking as though they rule from heaven, they lay claim to all that is on earth! Minions devoted to them suck up all that gets in the way of their consuming greed. "How does God know? The Most High has never inter-fered with us!" they declare.

I encourage you, take a good look at the wicked! As you said, they live at ease and easily increase in wealth.

So you looked. Contemplating the evident blessing on the wicked, you concluded, "In vain have I followed the ways of Jehovah. To no avail have I kept myself pure for Him. Every day, day by day, have I been punished and suffered plague for attempting to live in purity and righteousness in contrast to this world! Why have I restricted and withheld myself in light of what I see?" Frustrated, you realized that these thoughts were right on the verge of spilling out for everyone to hear! And you caught your-self. Had you poured out contempt for all that is good, you would have sided with the wicked! You would have betrayed the generation of God-followers. You couldn't make sense of this within your puny mind and life experience.

Then you came to your spiritual senses. You realized that true wisdom was much more than intellectual observation and evaluation. For then you came into My house, into My temple. You came into My presence! In My presence you could see those you held so highly, those wicked ones you longed to be like, from a different perspective. Now you could see their end!

Without a doubt I have put the wicked in a slippery place. Their ulti-mate crash is guaranteed. Their final desolation is a quick and horrible ending. They are utterly engulfed by their worst nightmare. The substance of the wicked appeal will vanish like a dream when I stand up and execute My judgment.

Looking back, you feel embarrassment at the longevity of your sour heart, your bitter spirit. It was as though a venomous serpent had pierced your heart with envy. You were like a wild, raging beast in My presence. You were ignorant, completely lacking true wisdom and understanding. Even in such a state of senselessness, still you were secure in My presence. Once *again you realize that nothing, not even your own raving, can separate you from My love.*

You're astounded at My gentleness in light of your crazed tantrum. I reach out and take your hand. Tenderly I lead you down My path of understanding, counsel, wisdom, and true knowledge. I've led you before. I lead you now. And I will lead you all the way to the finish line.

Now you see clearly. From deep within your soul your conviction erupts. Solidarity focuses you on the one thing you can count on: Me! You look up to heaven, and I am your deepest desire. You search earth and I am your only desire. And your satisfying awareness is that you not only desire Me but also can have Me!

Your body and heart may drag you down into the pit of failure, to the very brink of destruction. But I am the rocky summit of your heart. I am your portion. The wealth and security found in Me exponentially exceeds anything this world has to offer!

Those in rebellion against Me, those running the other way from Me, will finally be destroyed. But I get no pleasure in their doom. However, for you My very real presence is all you want. My nearness is all you need. I have become your safe place, your hiding place. Rest secure, My child. And keep your eyes on Me. You can't help but announce to all your friends the intensity of our relationship.

Reflections

It's so easy to spout religious platitudes about the goodness of God in our lives. Then behind the scenes we envy, grumble, and complain. Perhaps we have a misconception of true goodness. Obviously in God's economy, goodness is not void of suffering. Part of God's goodness is to use suffering and hardship to weave the character of Christ in us. J. B. Phillips renders James 1:2-3 this way: "When all kinds of trials and temptations crowd into your lives, my brothers, don't resent them as intruders, but welcome them as friends!" What is your typical response to trials and temptations?

In verse 2 of this psalm, we see that isolating ourselves from all other believers is actually a ploy of the enemy we tend to fall into. The more we gaze at the world, the more we drift from God. We see all believers in verse 1 experiencing the goodness of God. But then comes the dangerous phrase: "But as for me . . ." "I'm different from everyone else" is the first step down the slippery slope of self-pity and disaster. The misleading finale is comparing ourselves to the wicked. This is a lose-lose scenario. No one wins. Yet we all do it.

It can appear that those who cheat oftentimes win. Those who dominate others get promoted. Those who mock and ridicule all that is good and righteous succeed. Those who ignore the suffering of others don't suffer. Those who disregard the hungry are well fed. Those who mock God and heaven are promoted to leadership. We feel like screaming, "God, don't You see? Don't You care? It isn't fair!"

We may conclude with Asaph, "In vain have I kept my heart pure!" (v. 13, NIV). And without a critical realignment of ourselves to God, we may even join the ranks of the wicked. But when we come into the presence of God (a privilege that is always available), an entirely different perspective washes over us. We see the demise of the wicked. Perhaps not in the timeframe we would desire or expect, but we see their undoing nonetheless.

In God's presence we also face a necessary assessment of ourselves as we look longingly at the wicked. Identifying with the psalmist, we might say we were "senseless and ignorant . . .

a brute beast before you" (v. 22, NIV). This is a very honest and sincere estimation when we consider our ranting against God in light of the drama unfolding from Psalm 73.

But—"Whom have I in heaven but You? And besides You, I desire nothing on earth. My flesh and my heart may fail, but God is the strength of my heart and my portion forever" (vv. 25-26). This is always a good yardstick to return to for adjustment and realignment.

Is God really all you want? Is He really all you need? Is He your one desire? Of course not! Not all the time! With our wandering eyes and greedy hearts, we are all just like the psalmist. We too must return to the temple (our hearts—1 Corinthians 3:16) and make the necessary corrections as we see things more and more accurately from God's perspective.

Practice

Writing Prompts

» Remember to ask, "Lord, what would it sound like if You spoke this psalm to me personally?" Then take a moment to listen in silence.

» Suppose God said something like, "Of course I'm good to Israel; I chose them. But I am also good to . . ." Can you continue this phrase from verse 1?

» For verse 2, consider God's presence in these troublesome observations: "I was standing right there, never leaving your side, while your gaze was focused in the wrong direction . . ."

» Consider God's response in verse 11: "They obviously don't know much about Me. All knowledge resides with Me. They are barking up the wrong tree! I know their every thought before their troubled mind spews it out for all to hear."

» For verse 13, contemplate God's possible encouragement: "Don't give up! The wicked and arrogant are not your only option for evaluation. Remain pure. Maintain innocence. The race is not over yet."

» In verse 17, hear Him say, "Welcome home! Welcome to My house. Can you see more clearly now?"

» In verse 23, can you hear God say, "Oh how I wish you could keep this perspective. I'm right here. I haven't gone anywhere. In the midst of your envying, craving, and coveting, I've walked with you"?

» Enjoy rewriting the rest of this psalm in the first person!

Devotional Thoughts

» Do you tend to spout correct doctrinal belief about God when you feel just the opposite? What is the benefit (if any) of stating correct belief (such as "surely God is good . . .") even when you don't feel like it?

» Can you identify with verse 2—"My feet came close to stumbling"—as you compare your life to that of the wealthy and arrogant?

» How much of verses 4-12 remind you of your own comparison of your life to those who seem not to suffer?

» Have you ever felt, as the psalmist did in verse 13, that it really is of no benefit to have kept yourself pure? Recall a story when you went too far down this trail.

» To what extent can you relate to verse 17, that everything came into proper perspective when you entered the presence of God? Or are you remaining in a state of self-pity, comparing yourself to those seemingly better off? How can you follow in the psalmist's footsteps in altering your perspective from the world back to God?

» Engaging in the context of this psalm, can you say as the psalmist did, "Whom have I in heaven but You? And besides You, I desire nothing on earth. My flesh and my heart may fail, but God is the strength of my heart and my portion forever"? Perhaps this could be your prayer of adjustment in the weeks to come as you seek to return to God with your whole heart.

CHAPTER 13

PSALM 81

Do You Listen to God?

Psalm 81 (AMP)

SING ALOUD to God our Strength! Shout for joy to the God of Jacob!

Raise a song, sound the timbrel, the sweet lyre with the harp.

Blow the trumpet at the New Moon, at the full moon, on our feast day.

For this is a statute for Israel, an ordinance of the God of Jacob.

This He ordained in Joseph [the savior] for a testimony when He went out over the land of Egypt. The speech of One Whom I knew not did I hear [saying],

I removed his shoulder from the burden; his hands were freed from the basket.

You called in distress and I delivered you; I answered you in the secret place of thunder; I tested you at the waters of Meribah. *Selah* [pause, and calmly think of that]!

Hear, O My people, and I will admonish you—
O Israel, if you would listen to Me!

There shall no strange god be among you, neither shall you worship any alien god.

I am the Lord your God, Who brought you up out of the land of Egypt. Open your mouth wide and I will fill it.

But My people would not hearken to My voice, and Israel would have none of Me.

So I gave them up to their own hearts' lust and let them go after their own stubborn will, that they might follow their own counsels.

Oh, that My people would listen to Me, that Israel would walk in My ways!

Speedily then I would subdue their enemies and turn My hand against their adversaries.

[Had Israel listened to Me in Egypt, then] those who hated the Lord would have come cringing before Him, and their defeat would have lasted forever.

[God] would feed [Israel now] also with the finest of the wheat; and with honey out of the rock would I satisfy you.

I was "minding my own business," reviewing Psalm 84, when my eyes drifted across the page to engage with Psalm 81, a psalm unfamiliar to me. God's heart-cry that we would listen to Him jumped off the page. I'm always blessed and amazed when God takes initiative like this. Sometimes I choose the psalm. Other times God chooses for Himself. Or does He always choose, and I am just unaware?

Psalm 81 in the First Person

Sing for joy to Me, the mighty and powerful God of your strength! Shout out loud and express your joy to Me, the God of Jacob! Raise a new song; get the instruments out. Everyone sing at the top of your lungs and get those instruments jamming—timbrel, lyre, harp, trumpets, trombones, woodwinds, and strings. This is a major celebration! It's a day of feasting. We are celebrating the world-renowned rescue of My people from the clutches of Egypt. Let Me hear how happy and grateful you really are! I removed the heavy burden from your shoulders. Egyptians required less straw, more bricks. But I released your hands from the basket. You cried out to Me in your distress and I listened. I heard you! But I didn't just hear you—I responded! I answered. I came to your rescue. I spoke to you out of thunder. I tested your faith and your relationship with Me in deep waters. Now consider this: You cried out to Me, and I listened. But do you listen to Me? No! Oh, how I wish you would listen to Me, My precious people. Somehow you have concluded that this communication is a one-way street from you to Me. That sounds like a monologue to Me. I prefer a true dialogue with you. It is critical that you hear Me and listen to Me. I will not tolerate foreign gods among you. I alone am God, Jehovah, Yahweh. I will not share My glory with anyone. Worship Me and not the gods of your neighbors. I am the One who brought you out of Egypt, not those foreign gods. But sadly, you would not listen to My voice. You would not obey Me. It grieved Me to do so, but I allowed the stubbornness of your own heart to rule you. You lived with the consequences of your choices. Oh, how I long for you to listen to Me. That you would live in the ways and patterns I have made clear! If you would just listen to Me, how quickly I would defeat your enemies. I would deal with them rapidly and completely. We could partner together in war like never before. Those who hate Me would be vanquished. But you, My precious ones, would feed on the finest of breads and that amazing wild honey. I would fulfill your cravings if you would only listen to Me. After all, I listened to you.

Reflections

A celebration is in process. Singing, dancing, and good food are called for. In years past, God had rescued His people from the grip of Egypt. Now, ongoing festivities commemorate the historical deliverance from generation to generation. God's people should never forget the Exodus. The world should never forget the Exodus!

Israel didn't refer to the people God rescued as "them," but as "us." They identified personally and corporately as God's people, coming from the root of Abraham (Isaiah 51:1-2). And today, "we" are the people of God (1 Peter 2:9-10)! This is ownership and identity. Can you embrace this identity more personally?

When God's people cry out to Him for help, they (we) expect God to answer. And in this psalm, we see God not only hearing but caring; not only caring but answering; not only answering but responding profoundly with rescue. God does all and more than His people hoped for.

But it seems as though once the people of God (that's us) get what they need from Him, they drift away relationally. The elation following a rescue keeps us praising for a while, but soon we slide back into spiritual complacency. Life seems good. We don't "need" God immediately, so we don't strive to connect with Him (Deuteronomy 6:10-15).

But not so with God! In Psalm 81, He seems to say, "I listened to you. I sure wish you would listen to Me." In verse 7, He rescues His people. Three times in the span of verses following that rescue (vv. 8, 11, 13), in one way or another God says, "Oh, how I long for my people to listen to Me." Do you get the sad picture? The people of God are crying out to Him for deliverance! God answers with profound rescue—and then His people hang up the phone.

I can practically feel the emotion of Abba as He expresses His longing for us to listen and care. I'm reminded of a story a friend shared with me. He had visited his wayward son for the afternoon. As my friend was about to drive off, his son ran out to catch him. My friend's heart jumped as he anticipated his son saying, "Thanks so much for coming over, Dad! I really enjoyed our visit." Instead the son said, "Dad, could you give me twenty dollars?" My friend's heart sank as he pulled out his wallet. Is this how we treat God? Do we only come to God when we need something? Or do we genuinely give God relationship? After all, Father, Son, and Holy Spirit paid the greatest and most horrible price to purchase one thing: relationship. They wanted a relationship with you and me! Do we give them the relationship they want and deserve?

Practice

Writing Prompts

» Meditate on the first half of this psalm, verses 1-6. Can you get in touch with this historical celebration established by God Himself? He doesn't want His people to forget His most amazing rescue operation ever.

» Now, beginning with verse 1, enter into God's perspective: "Sing! Shout! Get your instruments out! Let's celebrate our rich history of rescue. Your oppression by the Egyptians . . ."

» The second half of Psalm 81 seems to represent a monologue from God's perspective. Sometimes we think, *It sure would help if we could actually hear Him expressing His heart like this.* Yet, is this psalm not the revealed heart of God? Can you receive this psalm as the currently spoken words of God?

» Can you engage with the possible emotions of God as He responds to the relational negligence of His people? "My heart was broken once again by you . . ." (v. 8).

» The second time God expresses His longing for relational connection is in verse 11: "Not only do you turn your back on Me after My rescue and response to your cries for help . . ."

» Verse 13 is the third and final plea of God for His people to engage with their hearts. Then in verse 14, He goes on to unveil how He longs to bless them, if they would only listen to Him: "I long to pour out blessings on you if only . . ."

» Enjoy rewriting the rest of this psalm in the first person!

Devotional Thoughts

» Unpack verse 7, considering all the dimensions of God's thorough response to the cry of His people. Look at all the angles of God's response to His people.

» Put yourself in the shoes of one to whom God is beckoning to listen to what He has to say (vv. 8, 11, 13). Enter into the relational attraction as God expresses His desire for your focused attention. Consider this question: "Typically when you come to Me, you do all the talking. Would you reconsider having a dialogue instead of your normal monologue?" How would you respond?

» Do you find yourself in one of these monologue quagmires, doing all the talking and not listening to God? Can you receive and engage with the heart-cries from God in this psalm for greater conversational oneness? Express your own sadness and commitment to God to change this pattern.

CHAPTER 14

PSALM 84
Well-Worn Paths to God

Psalm 84

How lovely are Your dwelling places,
O LORD of hosts!
My soul longed and even yearned for the courts of
    the LORD;
My heart and my flesh sing for joy to the living God.
The bird also has found a house,
And the swallow a nest for herself, where she may
    lay her young,
Even Your altars, O LORD of hosts,
My King and my God.
How blessed are those who dwell in Your house!
They are ever praising You.

How blessed is the man whose strength is in You,
In whose heart are the highways to Zion!
Passing through the valley of Baca they make it a spring;

The early rain also covers it with blessings.
They go from strength to strength,
Every one of them appears before God
     in Zion.

O LORD God of hosts, hear my prayer;
Give ear, O God of Jacob!
Behold our shield, O God,
And look upon the face of Your anointed.
For a day in Your courts is better than a
     thousand outside.
I would rather stand at the threshold of the
     house of my God
Than dwell in the tents of wickedness.
For the LORD God is a sun and shield;
The LORD gives grace and glory;
No good thing does He withhold from those
     who walk uprightly.
O LORD of hosts,
How blessed is the man who trusts in You!

Psalm 84 has become an old friend through the years. "Well-worn paths in my heart" is a beautiful translation for a portion of verse 5. Some translations leave verse 5 less picturesque. Others open up a view of walking with God on paths that become highways into His presence. May we not neglect the care and attention these paths deserve and need to enhance privileged time alone with God. And may we be drawn into the paths of your hearts with God just as He desires to explore these paths with us.

Psalm 84 in the First Person

I hope you enjoy My home! It's one of My ultimate successes, My magnum opus of dwellings. No extravagance was spared in the construction and design. Welcome home. Enjoy. Make yourself at home. It's your new home too. I know your soul longs for, yearns for, and is incomplete without a special place in My courts. Your heart, your soul, even your body sings with deep joy to Me, the only true living God, your God.

Birds make safe nests in nooks and crannies hidden throughout My house. Their young are born there and return to make family nests of their own. Their lovely voices add depth and harmony as you sing praises to Me. How blessed, happy, fortunate, even to be envied are those who dwell in My house. My presence naturally draws expressions of praise from all hearts and lips.

How blessed, happy, fortunate, even to be envied are those who find strength, power, a fortress, even a stronghold deep in Me. Here you are truly safe. In your heart I walk by your side, creating well-worn paths into My privileged presence. Walking with you in the depths of your heart, I reveal the hidden paths to the top of My mountain. There are no weeds overgrown on these paths because we tread them often together. These paths become highways up My mountain, Zion. Passing through the valley of weeping, I make it a place of life and nourishing springs. Gentle rains keep pleasant pools full of fresh water. As you travel these pathways in your heart with Me, to Me, your strength increases and multiplies beyond your wildest imagination. You experience the mystery of My strength living in the midst of your weakness. My power is perfected in your weakness. The journey is certainly enjoyable, but the destination, the summit of My holy mountain where our hearts entwine, you basking in My presence, is beyond compare.

I am Jehovah, the God of the hosts of heaven. Your prayers permeate

My presence. My ear is attentive to your voice. I see your shield, ready for battle! I see your face, watchful and alert. You are My anointed. One day in My courts, in My magnificent presence is better than thousands of days in the most perfect of settings away from Me. You would be much better off scrubbing floors in My house than dining luxuriously in palaces of sin, even in the finest castles of the world. But I certainly don't expect you to scrub floors in My house. Heavens no! I have a place of honor for you here. I am your sun, your warm radiance. I am your shield, an impregnable barrier. I am your grace and glory. I give good things to you as you travel these heart-paths with Me. Walk with Me and enjoy riches and benefits. All good things are yours; nothing is withheld. Trust Me! You are truly blessed.

Reflections

Is it boastful for God to talk about His house like this? Not at all! He is wooing us into the most fantastic dwelling ever conceived. Our souls ache to be in His presence (consider Psalm 27:4). Our hearts hurt with longing and desire. Only in Him are our deepest, true selves genuinely satisfied. But do we even know ourselves well enough to realize that this is mysteriously our deepest longing? If I'm honest, I have to say I don't always have this as my highest desire. But the more time I spend with Him, the more I genuinely long for more time with Him. The more my true desire is satisfied with authentic relationship with Him, the more diminished my earthly desires become.

Verse 5 has become one of my favorite engagements with God in the entire Bible. I used to walk the paths of a nearby state park once a week, spending extended time with God early in the morning. God and I met there to resolve the issues of life and to simply be together. I truly was drawn into ever-increasing familiarity and comfort of relationship with God in this special place. This park became my sanctuary. It seemed like God had set the park aside for our private walks.

Then life became more demanding. The "well-worn paths" in my heart became a luxury I felt I couldn't afford. Weeks slipped by without me walking the familiar trails with God. No more pauses in the woods observing His handiwork all around. No more silence as I perched on the boulder at the foot of my waterfall. Normal patterns of relationship with God became vague. Even though daily time with the Lord was still somewhat intact, my special extended times in the park suffered. Business with responsibilities had replaced process-ing life with the Creator of life.

My eventual return to early morning walks with God in the park occurred in the fall. Fall is such a stark season. Trees were bare. The lake that once poured over a small water-fall was still and stagnant. The stream that flowed from the waterfall was all but dried up. Small pools of murky water smelled of death. Once-clear paths through the woods were overgrown to the point of becoming obscure and hard to dis-cern. As I walked the old path, a penetrating sadness filled my soul. The image of my own heart-path paralleled the wooded path. Was this fall season in the woods reflective of the condi-tion of my heart? Were the well-worn paths in my heart dried up and overgrown?

God extends to us the high privilege of relationship in His presence. May we not neglect our private walks with Him. What could be more important?

Practice

Writing Prompts

» Meditate on verses 1-4. Read in several translations until you gain a good sense of God's heart. At times, I write from the contrast between Old and New Testaments. Consider this possible beginning (remember, this is God speaking): "For the psalmist, My dwelling place was a physical structure. But for you, pause and consider where I dwell today. I am always with you. I will never forsake you."

» Reflect on verse 5. Imagine God forming a well-worn path in your heart that goes up the mountain of God. Allow God to paint and embellish this profoundly relational reality being offered to you. At first, write from the point of view of your perceived heart condition, whether good or not so good. Then be sure to switch to the genuine truth that there really is a path in your heart that you and God walk together. Ponder this beginning: "I walk this path of your heart often. Sometimes you walk with Me. But many of My walks are alone. Just because you can't see Me doesn't mean I'm not here. Won't you join me? We could walk together as often as you like."

» Enjoy writing the rest of this psalm in the first person!

Devotional Thoughts

» Trust God to draw you into greater relationship through this hidden treasure of "heart-walks with God."

» Do you normally think of God's dwelling place as way off in heaven? Can you grasp and entertain the current reality that you are His dwelling place (see 1 Corinthians 3:16 and 6:19-20)? How would you decorate and design the perfect dwelling for you and God to enjoy together? Consider the kind of touches that would enhance your relational connection with God. What kind of personal touches do you suppose God might want?

» Another very familiar phrase to many is, "A day in Your courts is better than a thousand outside" (v. 10). But the next thought—"I would rather stand at the threshold of the house of my God than dwell in the tents of wickedness"—suggests a very interesting contrast. Write your own description of dwelling just outside the door into God's presence. Now write your description of dwelling in the opulent tents of the wicked. Would you agree with the psalmist's comparison?

CHAPTER 15

PSALM 91
Unusual Protection

Psalm 91

He who dwells in the shelter of the Most High
Will abide in the shadow of the Almighty.
I will say to the LORD, "My refuge and my fortress,
My God, in whom I trust!"
For it is He who delivers you from the snare of the trapper
And from the deadly pestilence.
He will cover you with His pinions,
And under His wings you may seek refuge;
His faithfulness is a shield and bulwark.

You will not be afraid of the terror by night,
Or of the arrow that flies by day;
Of the pestilence that stalks in darkness,
Or of the destruction that lays waste at noon.
A thousand may fall at your side
And ten thousand at your right hand,

But it shall not approach you.
You will only look on with your eyes
And see the recompense of the wicked.
For you have made the LORD, my refuge,
Even the Most High, your dwelling place.
No evil will befall you,
Nor will any plague come near your tent.

For He will give His angels charge concerning you,
To guard you in all your ways.
They will bear you up in their hands,
That you do not strike your foot against a stone.
You will tread upon the lion and cobra,
The young lion and the serpent you will trample down.

"Because he has loved Me, therefore I will deliver him;
I will set him securely on high, because he has known
        My name.
"He will call upon Me, and I will answer him;
I will be with him in trouble;
I will rescue him and honor him.
"With a long life I will satisfy him
And let him see My salvation."

In the first two verses of this psalm, God uses four distinct names for Himself. Then in verse 14, He expresses that His blessings come because we know Him by name. God wants to be known intimately, relationally. Do we only know about Him? Is our knowing limited to knowledge and information? Or do we truly experience Him by His specific names? Consider that each of the names God chooses for Himself throughout Scripture represents an invitation to know Him better by that specific name. We could spend a lifetime probing this depth and intimacy of relationship hidden in the names of God. The psalm goes on to describe a dangerous existence in a violent world. But God's people have a special covering of protection from Almighty God. Not so for the wicked.

Psalm 91 in the First Person

I am the Most High. Take up residence in my secret place.

I am the Almighty. Rest secure in My shadow.

I am Jehovah. I am your refuge, your stronghold.

I am your God! Trust in Me!

I will certainly rescue you from dangerous, hidden traps.

I will certainly rescue you from deadly threats.

Come close. Imagine Me as a mighty eagle. I will cover you with the strength of My wings.

You can seek safety under My outstretched wing.

My faithfulness and truth form a huge shield for you to hide behind.

They are your strong wall of protection.

You need not fear the dreaded terror of nighttime.

Nor should you fear arrows shot in daylight, or

Devastating disease that stalks in darkness,

Or disaster that strikes at noon.

These plagues will affect thousands around you,

at your side, at your right hand, and at your left.

But it shall not draw near to you.

You will see with your own eyes the retribution of the wicked.

For you have made Me, Jehovah, Refuge, Most High your dwelling place, your home.

No evil will overtake you.
No plague will come near your dwelling.
Because I will command My mighty angels concerning you
To guard you and protect you in all your ways.
Warring angels will lift you up
Lest you strike your foot on a stone and fall.
You will walk upon the lion and the cobra,
The young lion and the serpent you will trample down.
Because you sincerely love Me,
For this reason I will deliver you.
I will set you securely on a high vantage point
Because you genuinely know My name.
When you call on Me, I will answer you.
I will be right by your side during trouble.
I will rescue you and honor you.
I will satisfy you with a long life.
I will let you see My thorough and complete salvation.

Reflections

I love how God reveals Himself in the beginning of this psalm: Elyon (Most High), Shaddai (Almighty), Jehovah (LORD), Elohim (God). He extends to us such a personal and intimate invitation to know Him more deeply!

Then, through the metaphor of a young fowl, we are beckoned to seek shelter under His wings. Imagine the warmth and protection of a baby bird covered by the soft down of the underside of a mother's wing. The hunter's snare is an eminent danger. Pestilence is a reality the fowls face. Yet the young bird is safe from it all under the pinions of the strong wing. The baby is unaware of the threat to his very life. He is safe until he must learn to fly and fulfill his existence and purpose.

In the world, there is plenty of reason to be afraid, yet God says we are safe and secure because we know Him personally and we love Him. Draw near to your Mighty Protector. Receive His promise of profound protection and security. Don't take for granted God's ongoing defense, but thank Him for His constant guard over you.

Honestly, a troubling part of this psalm for me is God's promise in verses 5-8 that the destruction that falls on others (specifically the wicked) will not fall on the godly. Then I consider the destruction experienced by Job, a righteous man! I've seen inexplicable destruction fall on God's people. This is one of the mysteries of God that I just don't understand. I would like to believe that this psalm is God's promise to His people. Yet He does lift His protection at times, allowing destruction to fall on the unsuspecting. All of Job's friends were stupid. God trashed their reasoning in the end. Far be it from me to attempt to know or reveal the mind of God when mysterious catastrophes befall friends. When such a time comes, I hope I will weep with those who weep and mourn with those who mourn. And perhaps friends will do the same with me. I'll never forget disaster and death falling on the son of a dear friend. My friend had been raised in a very strict, legalistic religious context. Grieving beyond understanding, he and his wife received friends and family at the funeral home. His uncle, knowing that the boy had left their narrow sect of Bible enforcers, leaned close my friend and said, "He got what he deserved." I told my friend that if I had been standing beside him, I would have punched his uncle in the face! The very idea!

How utterly arrogant to think that we know the mind and heart of God (Romans 11:33-36).

Practice

Writing Prompts

» Remember to always ask the question, "Lord, what would it sound like if You spoke this psalm to me personally?"

» After listening quietly to verse 1, imagine God saying something like, "You are welcomed to dwell in My shelter. I am the Most High God. None are higher than Me. If you dwell here, My shadow will cover you. I will be your refuge and fortress. But let's talk about what it means to dwell here . . ."

» In verse 2, once you are safe under God's wing, you can shout out for others to join you in this protected refuge: "I am your refuge and fortress. Trust in Me. Tell your friends, 'Come in here from the vulnerable place you are in . . .'"

» Use these words as a prompt for verse 7: "The wicked are falling to your left and right. Thousands are falling all around you. But you will only look on and observe their demise. You are still safe under My wing . . ."

» Consider this for verse 14: "Your sincere love for Me has connected with My heart. I will deliver you. You have explored My name in order to know Me better. I will set you securely on a high place . . ."

» Enjoy rewriting the rest of this psalm in the first person!

Devotional Thoughts

» Reflect on each of the names of God revealed in the first two verses. Considering particular circumstances of your life, write how you are drawn to each of these specific identities of God. It may help to cross-reference these names with other Bible passages that also use these names. Can you begin to see the mystery that God is progressive and deliberate in revealing Himself with distinct names?

» Reread verses 5 and 6. Are there ways in which you can adjust your perspective from allowing something to cause fear in your heart to dwelling under the wings of God Himself, who dispels fear?

» In what ways does this psalm elicit comfort and security for you? Are there ways in which you feel unable to receive comfort and security from God? Can you engage Him in further conversation regarding your struggle? Be sure to focus on the truth revealed throughout Scripture about who God is and who you are in relation to Him.

» Are there ways in which this psalm seems "out of reach" because of your circumstances? Overlay Psalm 23 with Psalm 91. Does Psalm 23 help to draw you into God's protective cover?

» As you seek God more and more earnestly, ask Him to bring these apparent conflicting perspectives together in His love.

CHAPTER 16

PSALM 92
Even in Old Age I Praise You

Psalm 92 (ESV)

It is good to give thanks to the LORD,
    to sing praises to your name, O Most High;
to declare your steadfast love in the morning,
    and your faithfulness by night,
to the music of the lute and the harp,
    to the melody of the lyre.
For you, O LORD, have made me glad by your work;
    at the works of your hands I sing for joy.

How great are your works, O LORD!
    Your thoughts are very deep!
The stupid man cannot know;
    the fool cannot understand this:
that though the wicked sprout like grass
    and all evildoers flourish,
they are doomed to destruction forever;

but you, O LORD, are on high forever.
For behold, your enemies, O LORD,
  for behold, your enemies shall perish;
  all evildoers shall be scattered.

But you have exalted my horn like that of the wild ox;
  you have poured over me fresh oil.
My eyes have seen the downfall of my enemies;
  my ears have heard the doom of my evil assailants.

The righteous flourish like the palm tree
  and grow like a cedar in Lebanon.
They are planted in the house of the LORD;
  they flourish in the courts of our God.
They still bear fruit in old age;
  they are ever full of sap and green,
to declare that the LORD is upright;
  he is my rock, and there is no unrighteousness in him.

This psalm is a reflection on the goodness of God, provoking worship, praise, instrumentation, and song. The works of God are on display, yet the simple trample through life, missing the beauty and the mystery of God's touch throughout creation. The godly are richly blessed that they might proclaim new songs of God's goodness and faithfulness.

Psalm 92 in the First Person

My communication lines are always open, never in disrepair. I love to hear you express gratitude to Me for all I've done.

It is beautiful and pleasant to thank Me.

It is beautiful and pleasant to sing praises to My name.

Yes, I am the Most High God.

It is beautiful and pleasant to announce My unfailing love each morning,

To declare My faithfulness each evening.

It is beautiful and pleasant to accompany such worship with the guitar, the harp, and the lyre.

When you contemplate all I have done, your heart swells with gladness.

Songs erupt from your soul, proclaiming the works of My hands.

And these are not ordinary works. These works of Mine are magnificent.

My deepest thoughts are wrapped around My great and wonderful works.

The foolish of the world tread clumsily through My display of glory all around.

The brutish lack insight and sensitivity to pause and consider the mystery of My wisdom.

The wicked sprout like grass, quickly, effortlessly, selfishly.

They flourish rapidly, leaving little trace of their existence —

Their tenure short-lived, their destruction inevitable.

But I am the everlasting God! I am on high, exalted for all eternity!

My enemies wilt and perish before Me.

All engaged in evildoing will be scattered to the wind.

But My chosen ones I exalt like a strong ox.

I anoint them with My oil of honor and recognition.

Their eyes look confidently, victoriously, down on their foes.

Their ears hear the victory chants of mighty warriors.

My godly ones will flourish like a palm.

They will grow powerful like the mighty cedars of Lebanon.

They are planted in the courts of My house.

They blossom in My gardens.

Even in old age, they will bear desirable fruit.
They will be full of life juices, fresh with green leaves.
They declare to all who would hear that I am upright,
A rocky summit, and in Me there is no injustice!

Reflections

Genuine worship and adoration, erupting as we see God's hand of mercy and grace in our lives, truly is beautiful and pleasant, both to us and to God Himself. As we pour over verses 1-5, old songs may come back to mind, and gratitude swells, spilling out in genuine thankfulness. We have so much to be thankful for. But if God stopped His blessings today, He has already done immeasurably more than we could ever hope or imagine, especially in light of the Cross. To limit God's goodness to the scope of our natural lives is profoundly restrictive. The Cross was enough—yet God did not stop with the Cross. His goodness pours over us throughout our relationships, throughout our pursuits, throughout our journeys. May songs accompany our grateful hearts.

But without attentive hearts, it's so easy to miss, to overlook God's works and blessings. It's one thing to see the foolish brutishly plundering through life with little appreciation for the handiwork of God. If believers join them with neglect for beauty, sadness floods the hearts of the sensitive. But God strengthens the godly that they might worship Him with renewed passion!

At a precise time during summer, a small patch of Indian paintbrush flowers pop out just inside the gateway to my office. Every day I anticipate further appreciating the fiery orange-red bursts of color in an otherwise dull setting. I consider digging them up and transplanting them to my garden. After all, they are growing wild, and mowers will cut them down eventually. Oh, to cultivate and nurture such beauty.

Practice

Writing Prompts

» Picture God seated on His throne in this wild context of continuous, beautiful, unified worship erupting from His people. Now imagine that you are one of His people at this worship celebration. You hear Him say, "I never grow tired or bored with these displays of love and adoration from you." Then His eyes fall on you. "Sing Me a new song, precious child . . ."

» In verse 4, hear the dialogue continue as you observe the magnificent works of God: "I can see that you are overcome by My works. Your happiness and joy explode into more worship. Let's reflect a little on My works . . ."

» Beginning in verse 6, the attention shifts to the simple-minded: "Can you believe that these dull-minded brutes miss such a glorious opportunity to worship Me? I pour out revelation all around them, but they trample through it in search of dark things to satisfy their wicked desires . . ."

» Enjoy rewriting the rest of this psalm in the first person!

Devotional Thoughts

» Reflect on verses 1-4, allowing your heart of thanks to overflow in songs and thanksgiving.

» Go for a walk in the woods. Stop at a beautiful spot. Take your shoes off. Pause and worship the great God of creation.

» Consider that the wonderful strength you enjoy was given that you might worship God with all your might. Could you worship and praise Him with increased freedom and little concern for your reputation? If you were completely free of prying eyes, how would you worship?

» I'll never forget asking my ballerina daughter how she would worship the Lord if she could worship freely. She replied immediately, "Oh, Daddy, I would dance!" Will you allow yourself this same childlike freedom to worship God with no restraints?

CHAPTER 17

PSALM 100
A Psalm of Thanksgiving

Psalm 100 (NLT)

Shout with joy to the LORD, all the earth!
  Worship the LORD with gladness.
  Come before him, singing with joy.
Acknowledge that the LORD is God!
  He made us, and we are his.
  We are his people, the sheep of his pasture.
Enter his gates with thanksgiving;
  go into his courts with praise.
  Give thanks to him and praise his name.
For the LORD is good.
  His unfailing love continues forever,
  and his faithfulness continues to each generation.

We find at least seven distinct ways to worship God in these five short verses! True worship should be an experience of our whole person. Standing in a pew, singing a few songs, and maybe, if the Spirit moves us, raising our hands—these things are a far cry from what is expressed in this psalm. Here we find the engagement of body, mind, heart, and soul as the psalmist reveals his passionate worship of Jehovah God. I am reminded of David dancing before the ark of God as the processional returned the ark to its proper place in the tabernacle of God (2 Samuel 6:12-18).

Psalm 100 in the First Person

Get ready for some mind-blowing worship! Because when you see Me and experience Me for who I truly am, you will not be able to contain yourself. Earplugs are available at the door for those with sensitive ears.

Let Me hear it now. Shout out loud! Let joyful noise erupt from the pure delight of your heart. All earth, join in at the top of your lungs! Let Me hear the harmony. Let Me hear the horns blast at highest volume. Allow Me to conduct this symphony of magnificence and magnitude. I love it when you worship Me in spirit and truth.

There is a significant form of worship that not many think about. As you do your work, whatever you put your hand to, do it for Me with your whole heart! Are you a stay-at-home mom? Are you a CEO of a company? Are you a leader of people? Are you a cook? Are you a teacher? You fill in the blank! Be glad in your service.

As you come into My presence, allow yourself to be swept up in singing praises from the depths of your heart.

Intimately know Me. Perceive, recognize, discover, probe the depths of My Person. And let Me know you in the same way! Know Me as God. Know Me as King. Know Me as Creator. Know Me. I am who I say I am. I am not the small god you conjure up in your imagination.

I made you. You did not make yourself. You are not one of those "self-made" people. You are My people. You are precious sheep under My watchful care. Rest secure in that truth.

Come on in! Don't be shy. Don't stand outside the gate! Just put one foot in front of the other. Enter My gates. Express your deepest thanks for who I am and for all I've done. Allow yourself to be overwhelmed with My presence.

Come further! Don't stop at the gates. Come into the inner courts with praise. Simply join the praise that beautifully surrounds My presence.

Clap your hands. Don't hold back! Throw your offering of thanks into the air! Bow down humbly as you pour out your thank offering and say My name. Bend your knee so I can lay My hand on your head in blessing.

I am good, pleasant, beautiful, and delightful. Be drawn into My center. I revealed Myself to Moses as good. Now I reveal Myself to you as good. Let My goodness surround you. Let My goodness embrace you. Let My goodness wash over you.

My unending, unfailing, incomparable love lasts forever. My faithfulness and steadfastness form a rock for you to stand on. From one generation to the next, genuine experience with Me is passed on. But it is passed on with enthusiasm and excitement! So be set free, be released to worship Me in spirit and truth!

Reflections

Every verse in this psalm is packed with clear and distinct expressions of worship of God. When was the last time you worshiped like this? So often, we get bogged down in mundane demonstrations of praise. Let's go back to the Psalms and learn how to worship God from one of the most sincere worshipers ever. Jesus said that the Father is actively searching for people who would worship Him in spirit and truth. Let's dig into the truth and be set free to worship God beautifully and power-fully. As we move into the inner court, let's allow ourselves to be impacted by God's presence. May worship be a natural response to genuinely coming into the very presence of the living God!

The Hebrew words used in this psalm to guide us in authentic worship require a full-person involvement. Not just your mouth. Not just your spirit. Not just your heart. But in a truly biblical way, we must worship God with our entire integrated being: body, soul, heart, and mind. Some who worship God in a more subdued way say, "I'm worshiping God in my spirit." But your spirit is currently connected to your body! Why not let them participate together?

In my limited understanding of Hebrew, root word pictures are combined to form more complex words and ideas. For example, the Hebrew word for hand is *yad*. And one Hebrew word for praise and thanks is *yadah*. So, to not use our hands in worship and praise is highly disengaging and limiting of our whole-person experience. *Yadah* is the word for "give thanks" in verse 4.

In verse 1, the phrase "shout joyfully" is the Hebrew word *rua*, meaning to cast or throw. Further, *rua* means to split the ears with sound or to raise a battle cry. Hence the need for earplugs as you enter! Verse 2 has *abad*, sometimes translated "worship." But perhaps the more accurate definition would be "serve or work." This immediately took me to Colossians 3:23: "Whatever you do, do your work heartily, as for the Lord rather than for men." Verse 2 also has *renanah*, a shout for joy or a ringing cry. It's interesting that verse 3 does not have a specific word for worship but rather a brief aside to consider our relationship

with God because all of this worship is happening in the context of a wonderful relationship with Him. Verse 4 reveals us
progressing through the stages of God's temple, from the gates,
to the courts, and further. We enter His gates with *todah*, an
extension of the hand. We enter His courts with *tihillah*, a song
of praise. The Hebrew *yadah* is how we give thanks in verse 4.
"Bless" is the Hebrew *barak*. This word gives the word picture
of kneeling before God in humility and receiving from Him His
hand of blessing for His child.

I hope you can see the beautiful and relational progression
of these words for worship. Movement from loud and raucous
worship into full consideration of our work being a demon-
stration of worship takes us beyond any limited understanding.
What an amazing relationship we have with our God!

Practice

Writing Prompts

» Hear God conducting the praise around His throne:
"Shouting, worshiping, singing! Let all earth join in—every
animal, every plant, every waterfall, bring your full expression
in unity around Me. I am Jehovah. I am Yahweh. Pour out
your hearts of worship before Me . . ."

» In verse 3, wrestle with these ideas: "I made you. You belong
to Me. You are My people. I am your Shepherd . . ."

» Find words to express the movement of worship: "As
you enter My gates, let your thanksgiving gush. You have

so much to be thankful for . . ."; "As you progress into My courts, let your praise increase . . ."; "But don't stop at My gates or My courts; come into My inner court for fullness of relationship. Let your worship rocket to a whole new level in My presence . . ."

» Enjoy rewriting the rest of this psalm in the first person!

Devotional Thoughts

» Determine to practice one of the more expressive words for worship found in this psalm for a period of time. And it's fine to begin in the privacy of your own home or closet. I'll never forget a well-known pastor telling the story of God asking him to dance! He replied to the Lord, "But Lord, I don't dance." Finally, in the privacy of his own home, he gave the Lord what He had been desiring: an original dance.

» We can't just pop into the presence of God and engage with deep, heart-altering worship. There is a necessary progression of entering His gates, then going further into His courts before stepping into that most holy place, the place where God actually dwells, behind the curtain. And all of this movement from gates, to courts, to inner court takes place inside you—you are the temple of God (1 Corinthians 3:16; 6:19-20)! Have you ever worshiped the Lord and remained in His presence for more than an hour, for more than a day?

As we spend hours and even days together in the presence
of God, genuine transformation beautifully floods our souls.
Jesus would periodically take the disciples away for extended
time alone with Him. Do you have this rhythm of extended
time with God built into your life?

» I encourage you to start with two or three hours devoted
to focusing on God. You can do it alone or with a few close
friends who also long for deeper connection with God. Pore
over this psalm slowly for ten or fifteen minutes. Don't just
read the words; engage in the reality that you are in the
presence of God. As the priest of your temple, enter His
gates, continue into His courts, come humbly into His inner
court. Soak in passages like 1 Chronicles 29:10-13, Isaiah 40,
Psalm 34, Psalm 136, Psalm 139, and Colossians 1:13-20. Lay
the filter of Psalm 100 and the unique expressions of worship
found there over one of these beautiful invitations into God's
presence. Relax. Enjoy. Lift your hands. Wave your arms.
Twirl in dance. Allow yourself to be set free in extended time
with God. Express your own thoughts as they erupt from
your inner being. Perhaps read some of these treasures in a
very loud voice. The angels flying around God's throne in
Isaiah 6 were shouting so loudly that their voices caused the
foundations of the threshold to tremble!

» Next you could try half a day with the Lord. Then you
could experiment with a whole day. As you taste and see
that the Lord really is good, your taste will only cause you
to want more.

CHAPTER 18

PSALM 103
Bless the Lord, O My Soul

Psalm 103 (AMP)

Bless (affectionately, gratefully praise) the Lord, O my soul;
and all that is [deepest] within me, bless His holy
name!
Bless (affectionately, gratefully praise) the Lord, O my
soul, and forget not [one of] all His benefits—
Who forgives [every one of] all your iniquities, Who
heals [each one of] all your diseases,
Who redeems your life from the pit and corruption, Who
beautifies, dignifies, and crowns you with lovingkindness and tender mercy;
Who satisfies your mouth [your necessity and desire at
your personal age and situation] with good so that
your youth, renewed, is like the eagle's [strong,
overcoming, soaring]!
The Lord executes righteousness and justice [not for me
only, but] for all who are oppressed.

He made known His ways [of righteousness and justice]
to Moses, His acts to the children of Israel.
The Lord is merciful and gracious, slow to anger and
plenteous in mercy and loving-kindness.
He will not always chide or be contending, neither will
He keep His anger forever or hold a grudge.
He has not dealt with us after our sins nor rewarded us
according to our iniquities.
For as the heavens are high above the earth, so great are
His mercy and loving-kindness toward those who
reverently and worshipfully fear Him.
As far as the east is from the west, so far has He removed
our transgressions from us.
As a father loves and pities his children, so the Lord loves
and pities those who fear Him [with reverence,
worship, and awe].
For He knows our frame, He [earnestly] remembers and
imprints [on His heart] that we are dust.
As for man, his days are as grass; as a flower of the field,
so he flourishes.
For the wind passes over it and it is gone, and its
place shall know it no more. But the mercy and
loving-kindness of the Lord are from everlasting
to everlasting upon those who reverently and
worshipfully fear Him, and His righteousness is
to children's children—
To such as keep His covenant [hearing, receiving, loving,
and obeying it] and to those who [earnestly]
remember His commandments to do them
[imprinting them on their hearts].

The Lord has established His throne in the heavens, and
    His kingdom rules over all.
Bless (affectionately, gratefully praise) the Lord, you His
    angels, you mighty ones who do His commandments,
    hearkening to the voice of His word.
Bless (affectionately, gratefully praise) the Lord, all you
    His hosts, you His ministers who do His pleasure.
Bless the Lord, all His works in all places of His dominion;
    bless (affectionately, gratefully praise) the Lord,
    O my soul!

What a beautiful announcement to worship and adore God! All of creation, both heaven and earth, are summoned to bless Him. But the individual soul of each worshiper is addressed first. God's profound forgiveness and elimination of everything associated with our sin is powerfully explained. The frailty of humans is revealed. But God's overwhelming love, not what humans have done or not done, is the focus here.

Psalm 103 in the First Person

Bow your soul and affectionately express devotion and gratitude to Me. Yes, bow your fully integrated body, soul, mind, and spirit, pouring forth deepest devotion to My holy name.

Bow your soul and affectionately express devotion and gratitude to Me, and always remember the value and advantages of knowing Me. Don't take the benefits for granted.

I forgive the guilt of your immoral failures. I heal all the diseases that plague you. I wrap My hands around you and lift you out of the pit imprisoning you, out of corruption, out of the entrance to hell. But I don't stop there—I give you value and worth by dignifying you with My unfailing love and compassion. I satisfy the full length of your days with good things coming from My rich storehouse of blessings so that the youth within you soars like the eagle with strength, beauty, and grace.

For the oppressed, I deal righteously and fairly. My judgments for them bring relief. I revealed My true self to Moses, My deeds to My people Israel. I am full of compassion and mercy. My anger lies dormant, not easily provoked. I have storehouses of unfailing love and mercy ready to pour out on you. I will not always accuse and struggle with you. My anger is short-lived in comparison to My overwhelming love for you. I hold no grudges. You remember these arguments, but I don't. Your sin is never the determining factor in how I deal with you. I am not like you. You deserve severe payment for your misdeeds, but that is not the reward you receive from Me.

Let Me ask you something: "Can you measure how high the heavens are above the earth?" I didn't think so. Well, that's a good way of expressing how dramatically I love you with My God-perfect love! Pretty much to infinity and back for those in awe of Me! And another question: "How far is east from west, sunrise to sunset, north to south?" Pretty mind-boggling, isn't it? Well, that's how far I have separated your sins from you! Your deeds, good or bad, do not measure you. You are evaluated based on how much I love you! And let's review that once again: "My love is incomparable! My love is incomprehensible! My love is safe and secure. And all My love is for you!"

You earthly dads have great compassion and care for your kids, right? Well, take that great compassion and care to an exponential factor—that is how I love you! You see, I know what you are made of. I'm the One who created you from dust. I am deeply aware of your predicament.

Humans are extremely fragile and short-lived. Here today, gone tomorrow, sort of like grass. Take a flower, for instance—today it pops up in all its splendor. Tomorrow, the wind and sun scorch the life from its tender pedals. Oh, but My love ... My God-perfect love is from everlasting *to everlasting, from eternity to eternity, from infinity to infinity! Can you measure My love? Rest secure in My love, all those who are in awe of Me. And My righteousness is right there, immeasurable, alongside My love. And it's all for you, beloved.*

I have established an eternally secure covenant relationship with you. Clear instructions have been spelled out for you to know how to live with Me in this covenant. Live in My instruction. Find security and direction for how to prosper as My child. These guidelines are not burdensome. They are life and peace.

My throne stands high above the heavens. My sovereign rule governs all creation. Mighty angels, bow down and affectionately express devotion and worship of Me—carry out every directive from your Commander in Chief! Heed every word from My lips!

Hosts of heaven, bow down and affectionately express devotion and worship of Me. Serve Me and do My will. And may every expression of the works of My hands bless Me, bow down, and affectionately express devotion and worship of Me. In every nook and cranny of My creation, everyone and everything bow down and affectionately express devotion and worship of Me. You too, beloved, from deep in your soul, bow down and affectionately express devotion and worship of Me.

Reflections

I've often puzzled over the expression "bless the Lord." How do I bless Him? Isn't He already thoroughly blessed? Does blessing Him involve worship? Words of adoration? A renewed dedication to be totally His?

The root of the word *bless* comes from the Hebrew word *barak*, which as we learned in the previous chapter means "to kneel or bless." I've chosen to borrow from the Amplified Bible's expansion of *bless* and incorporate kneeling as bowing down. Enlarging *bless* to these dimensions gives the action of blessing more life and engagement. Even as we praise God, we find ourselves bowing humbly before His presence—His hand extends to touch our heads in blessing.

The personal engagement with "my soul" creates a contrast with the larger call for heaven and earth to bless the Lord. It's beautiful how God does not neglect the individuals when all of creation is to receive the same call. Somehow His eyes of kindness and warmth fall on each of us.

As I moved into verses 11 and 12, I contemplated the absurdity of the questions—how far is east from west? How far are the heavens above the earth? These are easy phrases to overlook. But God is clearly dealing with aspects of infinity poetically as He removes my sin and guilt from my existence. This seems to go so far beyond forgiveness! God forgets my sin and wants me to live in that reality. This is often so hard from an earthly point of view, yet true fullness of relationship depends on our believing and receiving this truth as God extends the kind of forgiveness only He authors.

The statements "He has not dealt with us according to our sin. He has not rewarded us according to our iniquity" cause me to pause. If God had dealt with me according to my sin, if He had rewarded me according to my iniquity, my plight would be hopeless. But instead, I am more than forgiven—I am God's son! I am a fellow heir with Jesus! God really is the extravagant prodigal (in the true sense of the word: "lavish, excessive") Father. There is no reconciliation known to man that approaches His extreme love. In my humanity, I find it incomprehensibly hard to receive such exaggerated love and pardon. Yet I must also realize how

I hurt God by refusing His flood of love and mercy. He paid the ultimate price because He wanted me back in total, complete relationship with Him. Will I deny Him that pleasure? In order to bless Him, I am compelled to receive His overwhelming love and forgiveness.

Practice

Writing Prompts

» Imagine God's closeness to David as he summons every aspect of his being to bless the Lord. The man of God draws from the depths of his soul, his heart, his spirit to unify blessing and worship of the only true God. Now, hear God say, "I am blessed, very blessed, as you call on your heart and soul to bow before Me. Your body, your mind, your emotions are all integrated together in worshiping Me. Continue, man of God, woman of God, to call on every aspect of your existence to worship and bless Me . . ."

» The list of benefits begins in verse 3. We are told to never forget them. Can you hear God say, "My benefits have been from the beginning of time. My benefits are not just during your brief existence. I am the One who forgives all your sins. That alone is benefit enough! But I don't stop there. I am the One who . . ."?

» Verse 10 begins a potentially terrifying awareness of God not dealing with us according to our sins. Consider God's perspective: "If I had dealt with you according to your sins, we would not be having this conversation. But I sent My own Son to stand between you and My wrath against all rebellion so you wouldn't have to face that wrath. Ponder this lavish gift: I have not dealt with you according to your sins . . ."

» Enjoy rewriting the rest of this psalm in the first person!

Devotional Thoughts

» In your own meditation and examination of Psalm 103, how would you express with greater color the word *bless*?

» Take some time, at the invitation of verse 2, to name some of the Lord's benefits that you enjoy.

» The subject of God pardoning our sin is addressed extensively in verses 3 through 14. As you soak in this section, first express your deep gratitude for the Lord completely removing all remnants of sin from you. Structure your words throughout this group to capture more of the intricacy and thoroughness of God dealing with your sin.

» Verses 15 and 16 could be referred to as mankind's brevity, his frailness, his futility, his vulnerability. Expand this understanding of mankind's finiteness. Then overlay man's condition with God's great and perfect love.

CHAPTER 19

PSALM 121
Where Does My Help Come From?

Psalm 121

I will lift up my eyes to the mountains;
From where shall my help come?
My help comes from the LORD,
Who made heaven and earth.
He will not allow your foot to slip;
He who keeps you will not slumber.
Behold, He who keeps Israel
Will neither slumber nor sleep.

The LORD is your keeper;
The LORD is your shade on your right hand.
The sun will not smite you by day,
Nor the moon by night.
The LORD will protect you from all evil;
He will keep your soul.
The LORD will guard your going out and your coming in
From this time forth and forever.

This psalm is one of the beautiful songs sung by pilgrims traveling to Jerusalem, ascending the mountains to the city of God. Perhaps as these pilgrims approached the city from a distance, the mountains surrounding Jerusalem dimly began to come into view, increasingly becoming clearer and clearer. Journeyers would cry out to one another, "I lift my eyes up to the mountains!" A fellow pilgrim would shout back, "Where does my help come from?" Some of the elder Israelites would cry out in unison, "My help comes from the Lord, Maker of heaven and earth!" Further testimony would fill the air with confident expressions of the Lord's presence, His protection, and His power: "We are the people of God! Our God is the same God of Abraham, Isaac, and Jacob!" Their pride would swell as they recalled the goodness and deliverance of God throughout history. This same God is the God of all believers today. I invite you into the journey to the city of God.

Psalm 121 in the First Person

You lift your eyes up to the mountains, wondering where your help will come from. Those mountains are where I met with you in special ways, during special days. Your help doesn't come from the mountains, though. Your help comes from Me, Jehovah. I made those mountains! I made heaven and earth!

I will not allow your foot to slip as you climb treacherous paths to know Me better. And I don't sleep or slumber while you rest. I don't even take catnaps. I'm always on the lookout around you and around all My people. You can rest secure and safe due to My watchful eye.

I am your keeper. I am your shade on your right hand. The sun I made? It will not scorch you during searing days. And My moon, at night, will provide only soft light.

I will protect you from all evil. Your enemy is always on the prowl. But I will keep your soul. Yes, I see the effect deep within you of this oppressive, evil world. I will guard your going out and your coming in. I'm always with you! And I will be your guard from now on, even forever.

Reflections

Until I meditated in several translations, I didn't realize that verse 1 could be asking a sincere question: "Could my much-needed help come from the mountains?" But then verse 2 answers, "No! My help comes from the Lord." And by the way, He made the mountains!

I processed this entire psalm one morning as I gathered multiple translations around the kitchen table. My computer was in the shop, so I returned to the comfortable and familiar feel of bound texts of Scripture. Some were old friends, soft and faded. Others were stiff and crisp and new. The words of God flowed into my language and touched my heart.

Perhaps the mountain context of verse 1 flows into verse 3's danger of slipping while traversing challenging peaks. My wife and I love to hike the mountains of Colorado. At times, a false summit reveals a whole new path before we reach the top. The summit itself is often a unique and gratifying experience. The hours of grueling struggle over rocks and around switchbacks culminate in reaching the tip-top of the mountain. Three-hundred-and-sixty-degree views of the surrounding crags make the climb worth it. Then I remember Psalm 84:5: "How blessed is the man whose strength is in you, in whose heart are the highways to Zion!" An alternate translation is "in whose heart are well-worn paths to God." This imagery can help us as we navigate into the privileged presence of God.

The psalmist is facing not only terrain dangers but evil enemies who are always just around the corner. And not only that, but the weather poses threats with the heat and darkness. Through all of these obstacles, God is his protector, shield, guardian, and comforter.

Practice

Writing Prompts

» God is always mysteriously with us. He is never not with us! Consider this introduction to this psalm of ascents from God's point of view: "You are journeying to Me, to My holy mountain. Your pilgrimage is long and hard. There is not always a sense of My presence. But I'm always right with you. You look to the coming mountains and cry out, 'Where does my help come from?' Your help comes from Me, Yahweh! I made earth, and everything in it! I even made the mountains . . ."

» Consider the following beginning for verse 3: "I watch your every step, ready to balance you when you stumble . . ."

» Enter verse 4 with this perspective: "While you sleep, I will . . ."

» Hold on to this promise from verse 7: "There is evil everywhere. I will protect you . . ."

» Enjoy rewriting the rest of this psalm in the first person!

Devotional Thoughts

» Where do you look first for help? Is there someone who is always there for you? Do you have a fat bank account that provides the cushion you fall back on? Perhaps your own ingenuity rescues you time and time again. Even though there are reliable sources that become our go-to places for help, God is still your helper. Meditate on where you go quickly for help and how you may be overlooking a deeper engagement with God in the process.

» Mother Teresa said, "You'll never realize Jesus is all you need until Jesus is all you've got." This is a difficult statement to process when most of us don't live in a poverty-stricken environment. How do you think Mother Teresa's comment helps to define your reality of genuinely needing Jesus?

» Meditate on your needs compared to the needs of poverty-stricken people facing starvation in third-world contexts. Thank God for His provision. Perhaps this is a good month to begin financial support of orphans or those in dire need.

» Are you aware of enemies on the prowl? Even though our enemies may not be physical, intending to harm our bodies, we certainly have an evil enemy, the father of lies, who is bent on our destruction. Engage with God on the truth that He is right there when you go out and when you come in. He never leaves you. Add a few lines to your Psalm 121 reflection in light of His presence.

» Our three oldest grandchildren were with us recently to launch our inaugural cousin camp. The time was full of fun, adventure, games, good food, and memories. But each morning we began by exploring Psalm 121 together. In a week's time, our nine-, seven-, and five-year-old grandchildren memorized this entire psalm. Repeating it over and over throughout the week etched a secure place in each of our hearts. Perhaps you would consider committing Psalm 121 to memory. Where does your help come from?

Epilogue

I TRUST THAT YOUR hunger for more of God has begun to be satisfied. If you simply read this book without engaging in the Practice section, much more treasure is still waiting to be excavated. I hope that your heart and soul are attuned to the Father, Son, and Holy Spirit in a richer way. I pray that your listening, waiting, and journaling skills are honed to better hear the conversation with the only true living God as He initiates with you.

Now that you have finished *Speak, Lord*, you can take your newfound approach to greater relationship with God into the rest of Psalms. I recommend having a special journal dedicated to listening to Psalms in the first person. You may have recognized by now that returning to any psalm months later with fresh eyes and ears quickly results in a whole new experience of receiving that psalm in the first person. Your current season, struggles, highs, and lows will be woven into the fabric as you rewrite the psalm from this fresh perspective.

May your constant prayer be, "Lord, I want to hear Your voice. Would You speak to me from this passage of Scripture?"

You can apply the "first person" principle to many other contexts of Scripture as well. Consider the question, "Lord, what would it sound like if You spoke John 10 to me in the first person?" It might sound something like, "When I come to call My sheep out of the holding pen, I walk right up to the door and enter. I would never enter by some other treacherous way. Only thieves and robbers would do that! I am the true shepherd, and I always enter through the door. The doorkeeper knows Me. He opens the door quickly and welcomes Me inside. I speak, and My sheep hear My voice. I call each one by name and lead them out."

Enjoy the Lord as you continue your exploration of the Word of God, spoken intimately in the first person to your heart.

Appendix A

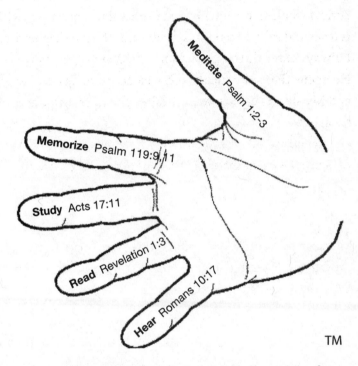

Meditate Psalm 1:2-3

Memorize Psalm 119:9,11

Study Acts 17:11

Read Revelation 1:3

Hear Romans 10:17

TM

HEAR

Romans 10:17

Hearing the Word from godly pastors and teachers provides insight into others' study of the Scriptures as well as stimulating your own appetite for the Word.

READ

Revelation 1:3

Reading the Bible gives an overall picture of God's Word. Many people find it helpful to use a daily reading program that takes them systematically through the Bible.

STUDY

Acts 17:11

Studying the Scriptures leads to personal discoveries of God's truths. Writing down these discoveries helps you organize and remember them.

MEMORIZE

Psalm 119:9, 11

Memorizing God's Word enables use of the Sword of the Spirit to overcome Satan and temptations . . . to have it readily available for witnessing or helping others with a "word in season."

MEDITATE

Psalm 1:2, 3

Meditation is the thumb of the Word Hand, for it is used in conjunction with each of the other methods. Only as you meditate on God's Word—thinking of its meaning and application in your life—will you discover its transforming power at work within you.

TM

The Word Hand illustration copyright © 1964 The Navigators. Used by permission of The Navigators. All rights reserved.